Endorsements

Within the pages of this fantastic book, Jackie Kendall passionately delivers with wit and wisdom a framework to help usher a princess into the arms of a committed prince, not a court jester. No fairy tales here, just biblical truth assisting dedicated families through discerning conversations and life skills which hold the potential to impact generations.

Michele Wetteland
Mom of five, children's author, and wife of New York Yankee World Series MVP, John Wetteland

This book cheers on girls after God's own heart. Jackie Kendall passionately fights for the hearts of young girls by sharing key principles which will guide tweens to make good choices and wait for God's best.

DeDe Kendall
Elementary assistant principal and co-author of *Lady in Waiting for Little Girls*

Jackie Kendall not only teaches this life message to guard girls from a Bozo and guide her to a Boaz—she also lives and breathes it with all of her inmost being and infectious energy. Jackie's passion, wisdom, and understanding, combined with her love for girls of all ages and her desire to see them walking in the truth of God's Word, propels this message in her newest book.

Vicki Rose
Author, speaker, and Jackie's prayer partner for 14 years;
wife of Bill Rose, Limited Partner
of the New York Yankees;
mother and mother-in-law of two very
precious women who waited

As a Christian therapist I regularly attempt to teach my single and divorced ladies to stop looking for Mr. Right but to use the "waiting room" time to focus on their own walk with the Lord. When a woman learns to love what the Lord loves, how could she help but be drawn to a Boaz who in many ways exemplifies Christ himself? And when she learns to love what the Lord loves, a Boaz couldn't help but be attracted to her—a woman whose eyes are fixed on pleasing the Lord. Only then can we see a true "love story from the Lord."

These are the principles Jackie so marvelously articulates in her book *Waiting for Your Prince.* Jackie's brilliant knowledge and love for God's Word, along with her love and devotion for the young girls she serves, shines through each page

Kathy Martin
Author of *God and Psychobabble*,
licensed clinical social worker

There is simply no greater investment you can download into your heart than the principles in this book! Having coached and counseled kids from the teens to the twenties for a quarter of a century, I assure you the anchor holds in these chapters. Besides that, I am living proof, having received one of Jackie's original manuscripts in 1988. No Boaz has had more prayer than mine. He has been well worth the wait, thanks to Jackie's teachings! As the pages turn you will find the time-tested skill set you need to design a Princess for King Jesus—a true Young Lady in Waiting.

Theresa A. Gernatt, "Coach Tag"
Former *Division I* basketball player and coach,
high school coach, and counselor

Having done Jackie's original *Lady in Waiting* study later in life, I can only wish that I had learned these principles at a younger age and avoided much heartache. I have lead the *Lady in Waiting* Bible study all over the country—with high school girls all the way to adult women—and have been blessed to witness the fruit in so many of their lives as they waited for their "Boaz" and are now raising children to know and love the Lord.

Kathy Edwards, RN
Traveling nurse in the NICU

Waiting for Your Prince is a must-read for all girls. I would read the phone book if Jackie wrote it! Her style of hard-hitting practicality mixed with insightful biblical truth always challenges me. Jackie has taken her *decades* of Bible study, mixed it with the time-tested truths she laid out in *Waiting for Your Prince.* This book will never make it to my bookshelf; it will stay prominently positioned on my bedside table as a constant reminder and reference point for our young daughter, and someday it will be on her bedside table.

Sami Cone
Founding blogger at SamiCone.com,
nationally syndicated radio personality,
TV's *Frugal Mom*,
author and conference speaker

As a mother of two young daughters and a college softball coach, I am thankful that Jackie Kendall has put to pen what the Lord has laid on her heart to provide a resource to help us encourage our daughters to seek after God's best for their lives. Young girls can learn practical ways to be empowered to wait for a prince of a guy who will treat them with love and respect and will truly be their Boaz. I married my Boaz seven years ago, a man of God who honors me and provides an amazing example of how a husband should treat his wife. I have seen how the principles of *Waiting for Your Prince* guide and inspire young women to wait for God's best. This book is certain to continue to positively impact lives for future generations!

Kimmy Bloemers
Head softball coach for Palm Beach Atlantic University;
daughter of Hall of Fame baseball player, Gary Carter

Waiting for your Prince

Waiting for your Prince

A
Message for the
Young Lady in Waiting

Jackie Kendall

DESTINY IMAGE® PUBLISHERS, INC.
P.O. Box 310, Shippensburg, PA 17257-0310
"Promoting Inspired Lives."

This book and all other Destiny Image and Destiny Image Fiction books are available at Christian bookstores and distributors worldwide.

Cover concept by: Prodigy Pixel

For more information on foreign distributors, call 717-532-3040.

Reach us on the Internet: www.destinyimage.com.

ISBN 13 TP: 978-0-7684-0535-4

ISBN 13 eBook: 978-0-7684-0536-1

For Worldwide Distribution, Printed in the U.S.A.

1 2 3 4 5 6 7 8 / 19 18 17 16 15

Dedication

To Ken, my Boaz for 40 years…

Acknowledgments

First and foremost I want to give all praise to my Lord and Savior, Jesus Christ, who birthed this message in the heart of a college freshman and allowed it to grow into a lifelong ministry of warning others to not settle for a Bozo, but to wait for a Boaz.

Second only to Jesus, I want to thank Ruth Olsen, my invaluable editor. Ruth made sure that my heart in print would be inspiring and not overwhelming to a precious Young Lady in Waiting.

My thanks as well to Ruth's special "tween" advisor on the editing project, Kelsey McLernon, who gave much great feedback on the manuscript.

Special thanks to the Destiny Image team that has championed the *Lady in Waiting* message for 20 years, taking it all over the world.

Last but not least, my husband, Ken, who has been my Boaz for 40 years and continues to be "a man worth waiting for."

Contents

Introduction

A Fairy-Tale Engagement

Do you know any stories about people getting engaged to be married? You know, the guy drops down on one knee, pulls out a diamond ring, and "pops" the question… the girl gasps and starts to cry, "Yes! Yes! I'll marry you!" Or maybe you've seen a video where they're at a baseball game when suddenly the jumbo screen flashes up a banner sign, "Britney! Will You Marry Me?" And the whole stadium bursts out in cheers as the camera then shows Britney, screaming, "Oh my goodness! Oh my goodness!" while her guy drops to one knee in front of thousands of people and slips that ring on her finger. Private or public, quiet or crazy, it's a very exciting moment in life! My engagement story happened sooooo many years ago—probably even before your parents got engaged—and it was one of the most perfect days of my life. Let me tell you about it!

My boyfriend's name was Kenny, and he was a very thoughtful guy. When he decided to propose to me, he put a lot of prayer and thought and effort into making our engagement one of the most treasured times of our lives together—and *wow* did he succeed! To this day when I remember all the special details he paid attention to as well as the ways that the Lord blessed that beautiful night, I still feel *so* grateful.

We were home on a break from college, and Ken made plans for us to drive to Disney World for the day. We lived in Florida, and Disney World was about a three-hour drive away. Just going to Disney World was a thrill for me—and do you know, it still is to this day! But Ken had much more in store than taking me up Space Mountain; he had called ahead and made reservations to take me to one of my favorite places in the world—Cinderella's Castle—and to a special restaurant inside the castle.

Can you even imagine how excited I was to walk through those doors and be escorted into the castle? I already felt like a princess with my handsome and kind prince.

Being taken to Cinderella's Castle at Disney World was only the beginning of the night's surprises. As we enjoyed the most amazing food in that magical place, suddenly a group of singing waiters came right up to our table, singing to us songs about our love and delivering one of my favorite deserts: cherries jubilee—that's the one they light with a flame as they deliver it—a very exciting presentation! As if this were not spectacular enough to this young woman in love with this wonderful young man, one of the waiters handed me with a beautiful book of poetry and announced in a loud voice, "A delivery from the prince of the palace!" It was a book addressed to "Princess Jacqueline."

And *then*, at what seemed to be the high point of this fabulous evening, our waitress asked, "Are you ready for me to take the picture?"

"What picture?" I blurted out, surprised again.

My sweet prince smiled at me and said, "She is going to take our picture out on the balcony overlooking the Magic Kingdom."

Well! If you think I walked, you'd be wrong, because I'm sure that I floated out onto that balcony. I knew full well that "no one" ever got to go to that special place—or, so it seemed—no one besides Cinderella waving at the crowds below. But there I was, and there we were; and before I knew it, the picture was snapped, the waitress left, and Ken Kendall turned to me and asked me to marry him.

Was this really my life? For a girl from a very unhappy family, fairy tales and daydreams were a common way for me to sort of "leave" the painful world I lived in and escape in my mind. When I was a girl your age, I would never have imagined that in such a magical place, such a good and kind guy like Ken would ask me to be his bride. And what was also *so* interesting was that Walt Disney himself was raised in a very troubled home. It was his dream to create a beautiful, fun, and safe place for families. Out of something painful in his life, he created something beautiful—Disneyland and Disney World. Out of something painful in my life, God was creating more beauty than I could imagine.

That very night when we were engaged, God gave Ken and me a special bonus that was like a shining star of *His* beauty. As we left the castle, we talked about our waitress, whose name was Jan, and how she was interested when we told her that God was at work in our lives. She even told us that she was trying to understand what she was supposed to do in her life, why she was on this earth. We shared as much as we could with her as she served our dinner, and now we decided to go back to the restaurant and tell her that we would love to talk with her more about God's purpose in life that she was searching for. When we walked back into the restaurant, Jan actually came running down the stairs to meet us! We sat in the lobby of Cinderella's Castle and shared with her the hope that we both had found in Jesus. She said, "You were so loving toward me, I knew there was something different about you both."

So that night, Jan bowed her head and gave her heart to Jesus as Savior and Lord. When we hugged her good-bye and turned to walk away down Main Street, Kenny and I were so excited! "We just got engaged, and God led us to share the love of Jesus with our waitress! We have promised our hearts to each other and Jan has given her heart to Jesus!"

It was the *perfect* ending to this fairy-tale night. Talk about double joy! We walked out of the Magic Kingdom just overflowing with joy.

As I write this book, I have been married to that sweet man for 40 years! In fact, that is partly the reason I am writing this book. I want to tell you about all the things God helped me to learn so that I would be *ready* to marry such a *prince* of a young man like Kenny. *You* may be many, many years away from getting married, but here is a secret about that far-off land called "marriage": You are taking steps on the journey to that land *today!* You might be 10 or 11 or 12 years old, but choices you make in your life *now* can lead to good choices when you are 16 or 18 or 25 years old. These are all the steps on the path to that future. Now, the title of this book is *Waiting for Your Prince*, and a lot of what I write here is about what the Lord taught me while waiting for my prince of a husband. However! Do you know who the *true Prince* is in your life? It is the Prince of Peace, Jesus.

In the Book of Isaiah, this is one of the titles for the coming Messiah—the Prince of Peace. So, the deeper meaning of this title is that we are always waiting first and foremost for Jesus. And that's not just a "hanging out" kind of waiting, but a kind of waiting that means "to look actively for" and "hope for" and "expect." I want you to picture what it's like when you are excited to see someone you love very much—maybe a parent coming home from a trip or a cousin or a grandparent you don't get to see very often coming for a visit. You look out the window and maybe even sit out on the front step, stretching your neck to see every car coming around the corner. Perhaps you go to pick them up at the bus station or airport and you watch on your tiptoes over the crowd to get the first glimpse of that person's face. Once he or she shows up, you *run* to them and grab them in a big hug! *This* is what it means to "wait" on

God. We want to be actively looking for what it is that God wants for us. We want to practice learning His Word and thinking about who He is, what He is like, and what His will is for us. We want to pray for that with enthusiasm. It's like our actions are saying, "Oh, God! I don't want to miss seeing you in the smallest areas of my life! So please show me what it is to think like You and act like You in all I do!"

As we learn about this kind of waiting on God, waiting and looking to see the Prince of Peace show us how to live our lives, we grow the best kind of heart attitude to "wait" for what God wants for us. From what you see on YouTube or TV or in the movies, you may think that girls are supposed to think more about finding the right pair of jeans or the coolest pair of shoes than picking the right kind of guy to date or man to marry. In this book, I am going to tell you about *two* kinds of young men that the boys around you might become as they grow up, as they make choices along the path of their own lives. And I am going to share with you some ideas that will help you grow in following Jesus *and* in your friendships with boys.

The ideas that you will read about are very important ideas. I like to think of them like signs on the road that help a driver to know which way to go *and* which way *not* to go.

It's like our actions are saying, "Oh, God! I don't want to miss seeing you in the smallest areas of my life! So please show me what it is to think like You and act like You in all I do!"

Do you ever pay attention to street signs when you are in a car or a bus? We all know how important that octagonal red sign is—you know the one: STOP! Can you imagine how cars would figure out who could drive through the intersection if there were no STOP signs? There are signs and there are rules for the drivers that are made to keep people safe. Some signs tell us how far it is to get somewhere, and some have warnings, like, "*Bridge is slippery when wet.*" So, street signs are put out to both *guide* a driver and *guard* a driver... and that is what my hope is for the ideas in this book. My hope for you is that you will learn about these ideas and that they will help you make the best choices, they will help to guide you along and also guard you on this journey toward the day *you* might be the princess getting engaged to her own prince.

I wrote above about the *journey* to getting married; but I want to make something clear: not everyone gets married. Many, many of you reading this book, probably *most* of you, will marry and have your own families (and if you already know you want that, it is a great thing to be praying for God to help you be ready for!). The *most important* goal of your life, though, is to become the person that God wants you to be and to learn to walk out the path *He* has for you. That is what the ideas in this book are written to help you with, whether your future is to be a wife and a mom with three kids *or* an astronaut who flies to Mars...*or* both!

Okay, girls! Are you ready for this road trip we will take together in this book? In a minute, I am going to tell you what the chapter names are—and don't worry! If you see words you don't know, I will explain those to you when you get there. First, though, I want to tell you about those two kinds of young men I mentioned, because you will see these words a lot in this book: *Boaz* and *Bozo*.

Kind of like a fairy tale, where there are good guys and bad guys, I came up with names that describe the best kind of guy and the worst kind of guy. In real life, people are really a mix of good and bad, aren't they? But in stories, characters are often shown as much more one side than the other so that we can see more clearly the things that make up the positive or negative. The Hero is often brave and strong, while the Evil Villain is tricky and mean. The best stories, in my opinion, are when the bad, or evil, guy gets changed and turns away from his evil ways. So, as you read this book and see the word *Bozo* (that's the "bad" kind of guy), keep in mind that it is good to recognize what a Bozo is like so you know to be careful in your friendships, but that we always want to pray for someone to be changed into the *best* version of themselves.

As I said, there are boys and young men I call *Bozos*—like Bozo the Clown, who was a very popular clown when I was growing up. These are the guys who are not serious about caring for others, who just "clown around" when it comes to learning about Jesus or about how to be a thoughtful, helpful, and brave man in life. The opposite of a *Bozo* is a *Boaz*. You will learn more about Boaz in this book, but he was a real person in the Bible. He was the good, kind, and brave man whom the Lord chose to marry the woman named Ruth. Maybe you know some things about the Book of Ruth in the Old Testament, but if not, you will certainly come to know about that Bible story by reading this book. That Bible story was hugely important in my life and taught me so many of the ideas I will share with you, so there was no question in my mind that the *best* kind of man who makes the *best* kinds of godly choices I would call a *Boaz*.

My young friend, my "little sister" in Christ, someone who loves you has given you this book or helped you buy it so that you could learn more and more about what it is to follow Jesus and get ready for the step-by-step journey of the best choices you can make in your life. Here are the chapter titles of the book, which include the main ideas you will learn about and grow in:

- Becoming a Young Lady of Total Surrender
- Becoming a Young Lady of Diligence
- Becoming a Young Lady of Faith
- Becoming a Young Lady of Virtue
- Becoming a Young Lady of Devotion
- Becoming a Young Lady of Purity

- Becoming a Young Lady of Security
- Becoming a Young Lady of Contentment
- Becoming a Young Lady of Conviction
- Becoming a Young Lady of Patience

Every one of these was an idea the Lord gave me as I studied the beautiful love story in the Book of Ruth between Ruth and Boaz. These were the road signs that guided me to my own fairy tale, the story I wrote in the beginning of this Introduction, and they can be a GPS to guide you to your own "happily ever after!"...so let's get going!!

Chapter 1

Becoming a Young Lady of Total Surrender

The safest place for your dreams is in God's hands. –JMK

Ruth's Total Surrender

I can think of no better way to begin telling you about road signs that will guide and guard your journey than to tell you about a woman who is very important to us and about *her* journey. That woman is Ruth, and I imagine you have learned about her in church, and hopefully even read the Book of Ruth yourself! To start with the "end" of the story, do you remember why Ruth is so important to Christians? Well, she was a woman chosen by God to be in the lineage of Jesus. Ruth was a great-great-great...great-great-great (keep going!) grandmother of Jesus. How she came into that line of ancestors is a story of great faith and true obedience to God—as well as being a wonderful love story!

At the very start of this Bible story we are introduced to a family that had faced a terrible crisis. There was a famine in Israel, and so this family fled to the land of Moab. The mother of this family is Naomi, and before the sixth verse of the chapter, ten years have passed, and Naomi finds herself and her two Moabite daughters-in-law tragically widowed. All three of their husbands had died. The one ray of light in this tragic situation was that the Lord had ended the famine in Israel; and so it was that Naomi set her path to return to her homeland, where her relatives would be and, as a widow, she would be cared for by them.

What a time of tough choices for these women who themselves had become family to each other in Moab! God's Word tells us next that Ruth makes an extraordinary decision. Ruth chooses to go *with* Naomi back to the land of Israel. She chooses to turn her back on her people, her country, and her gods. Let's really think about this. Ruth left the only life she had known. What on earth would have made her do that? Some might call it foolish for a young woman to leave her people with no hope to be re-married in a strange land. But here is the secret of that difficult decision: Her thirsty soul had tasted of the God of Israel by becoming part of Naomi's Jewish family; with just a "taste," she gives herself to the only true God by leaving her homeland of Moab and following her mother-in-law, Naomi. Ruth surrendered herself *to* something and to *someone.* She surrendered herself totally to the God of all Creation.

> *But Ruth said, "Do not urge me to leave you or turn back from following you; for where you go, I will go, and where you lodge, I will lodge. Your people shall be my people, and your God, my God"* (Ruth 1:16).

Can you hear the determination of Ruth's heart? As the story continues, we see that the Lord honors her faith in moving away from all that was familiar and taking a journey toward the completely unknown. Ruth did not allow her friends, her old surroundings, or her culture's dead religion to keep her from running hard after the only true God. She did not use the excuse of a dark past to keep her from a bright future that began with her first, huge choice—total surrender to the Lord God.

A "Shout *Yes!*" Girl Changed the World

How does a girl show her own "total surrender" to God? Does she have to leave her family, hometown, and all her friends to prove how serious she is about such a promise?

Well, occasionally God might ask that of someone, but most of the time she simply needs to wake up in the morning and shout "Yes!" to whatever the Lord has planned for her. To "give" your day to God is to totally surrender or give over you own ideas about what "should" happen or what "must" happen and to open your mind and heart to what God wants.

This "shout Yes!" method may seem simple, but it can be a real challenge. The Bible tells us a very important story, which you already know, about a teen girl who said "Yes" to God and was given the blessing of becoming the mother of Jesus, our Messiah. Young Mary was not chosen by God because she was "better than" all the teen girls in her neighborhood or youth group. Mary was chosen because God knew she would say *yes*. Here is that teenager's response to the angel Gabriel:

> *"I am the Lord's servant," Mary answered. "May your word to me be fulfilled." Then the angel left her* (Luke 1:38 NIV).

Mary was a teenager whose "Yes" changed the world. Now, in contrast to young Mary's "Yes" to a heaven-sent assignment, God's Word tells us about an old priest who, six months earlier, struggled to say "Yes" to his miracle when talking to that *same* angel, Gabriel (see Luke 1). Zachariah was not only an adult but a leader in the Temple, and he resisted the miracle God was promising—a child who would be given to Zachariah and his wife Elizabeth in their old age. This child was to be John the Baptist; but basically, Zachariah's words to Gabriel meant, "That's impossible!" Because he questioned God's plan and did not respond with a faith-filled "Yes!", Zachariah was struck mute until his miracle son was born.

> *And behold, you shall be silent and unable to speak until the day when these things take place, because you did not believe my words...* (Luke 1:20).

The angel Gabriel spoke with both an old priest and a young girl, and the young girl responded with total surrender to a most amazing and challenging assignment. Saying "Yes" to God is an act of daily, sometimes *hourly* surrender and it shows our willingness to act in faith and obedience. You are never too young or too old to shout "Yes" to Jesus!

Belle Said "*Yes*"

When I think of a girl who gave up family, hometown, and all her friends, I can't help but think of my favorite Disney movie, *Beauty and the Beast.* Remember the scene in the movie when Belle timidly said, "Take me"? She offered her life to free her dad, whom the beast had taken captive. I love that even in this Disney cartoon, we get to see a great example of "total surrender" when Belle gave herself as a prisoner to set her dad free—she said "*Yes*" and was willing to sacrifice much.

Let's return for a moment to the story where the angel Gabriel told Mary that she would be the mother of the Messiah. Here was a teenager who simply responded to the angel's amazing words, "You will be with child," with the most simple question: "How can this be?"

The angel answered her question by explaining, "What is impossible with men is possible with God."

And young Mary, who may have been 13 or 14 years old, answered in complete faith. To put it in more of today's language, it may have sounded something like, "OK, I'm in. Whatever. I'm His servant" (see Luke 1:31-38). In the Living Bible version, Mary said, *"I am the Lord's servant, and I am willing to do* ***whatever*** *he wants. May everything you said come true"* (Luke 1:38).

I love that a teenager said "whatever" to God. Mary's "whatever" was not at all snarky, though; instead, she was saying "*Whatever* God wants for me, I want to do." These were the words that showed her heart attitude was surrendered or yielded to God's will. This teenager didn't say, "Are you *wacked*?" She simply asked, "How is this possible?" And that was all right. It was an honest question. God loves our honest questions.

The "holy whatever" that Mary said to the angel Gabriel is a key to understanding the next story I want to tell you: The Secret of the Alabaster Box.

The Secret of the Alabaster Box

In the days of Jesus, when a girl was old enough to marry, her family would buy a beautiful box made of a shiny, white stone called *alabaster.* In those days, there were ointments (kind of like hand lotion or special oil) that were made to smell good by adding flower or plant oils. Both the box and the ointment were expensive, and the size of the box and the value of the ointment showed a family's wealth. The ointment-filled box was part of her dowry—the set of gifts and money that were given to the groom's family when the young couple married. When the young man came to ask for her hand in marriage (after it had all been decided by the parents), she would take the alabaster box and break it at his feet. This act was called "anointing," and doing this at his feet showed him honor and showed that the girl was making a promise to him.

In the Book of Mark (14:3-9), we can read an unusual story of what a woman did with her alabaster box. One day when Jesus was eating in the house of a man named Simon the leper, a woman came in, kneeled down on the floor by the feet of Jesus, and broke her alabaster box. She then stood up and poured the expensive ointment on Jesus' head. It is almost impossible to imagine an act in our time that would be like this, because it was much more than just giving him something of great value. But to even imagine *that* is helpful and gets us in the right direction to understanding what this woman did. So, imagine that your parents gave you some jewelry of real gold and real diamonds and told you to save them to give to the man you were going to marry as a promise that you would love him and a symbol that you gave all your dreams to him. Maybe it cost your parents more money than their car or even a house to buy this jewelry! Very special jewels for their precious daughter to give to her one true love.

The woman in the Bible who broke her alabaster box for Jesus was saying with her actions, in front of many other people, that *He* was her one, true love and that *He* was the man she would honor above all other men. This woman was honoring Jesus as Messiah, so to give her "all" to Him was the right thing to do. She wisely broke her alabaster box in the presence of the only One who can make a girl's dreams come true.

Amazingly, here is what Jesus said in response to her act of sacrifice and honor, *"Truly I tell you, wherever this gospel is preached throughout the world, what she has done will also be told, in memory of her"* (Matthew 26:13 NIV). The woman acted obediently in honoring Jesus, and He responded by promising that her unusual act would be remembered throughout the years to come. Not only would she be remembered as a person who acted in faith, but she would inspire millions and millions of people—even billions—to "pour out" ourselves to Jesus.

What is in your alabaster box? What do you "have" that is of great value to you that you would not want to give up? Maybe more important, what *hopes* do you have that you think you cannot be happy if they don't come true? All girls hold on tightly to their alabaster boxes of dreams. You may not yet have your mind set on boys or on finding a husband, but what about the dream of having a certain thing you want *so* much or the strong hope that someone will include you at school, pay attention to you, and want you to be her friend? We can have big dreams for the future, but also many smaller dreams that keep our minds busy every day.

Every kind of hope, wish, and dream needs to be poured out at the feet of Jesus!

Whatever dreams are in your alabaster box right now, when you've placed your alabaster box at His feet, you will be able to respond like Mary to a heaven-sent assignment. When Mary was asked to become pregnant while engaged to Joseph, she did not argue with the angel. Her response was that of a girl who had already broken her alabaster box at the feet of Joseph (her fiancé) and was now ready to take her broken box and lay it at the feet of a heavenly Bridegroom. She said, *"I belong to the Lord, body and soul..."* (Luke 1:38 PNT).

I share the alabaster box story to cheer you on as you give each of your dreams to God, over and over again. Dreams are what our hearts most want. They are what we think about and hope for. Too often, though, we set our minds on what we most want and think we *need* in order to be happy, without praying and asking God to show us His will. When we don't get that thing, or if the situation we want doesn't happen, we can be disappointed and even angry. When those feelings are practiced over and over in our minds and hearts, we can become *resentful*. The Bible has another word for when disappointment turns to anger and then resentment—bitter.

To be bitter and resentful is an awful way to live! It makes us and those around us miserable. So, what I want you to learn is how to notice what you are wishing for and expecting. You really can get better and better at noticing this—ask the Holy Spirit to help you! And then, whether it's winning a soccer game or getting an iPad or longing for a BFF, you can catch yourself and say, "Lord! This hope is in my box. I bring it to You and give it to You. I break this box at Your feet, Jesus, and trust You with this dream. Thy will be done!"

The safest place for your dreams is in God's hands.

Still Grinning from a Date with Jesus

With this image in mind about surrendering our thoughts and dreams to God, I want to tell you about another important thing I have learned about "waiting" on God. He wants us to spend *time* with Him, and to do that we have to make choices about our time that focus on the Lord *on purpose*. When I was a new Christian—at 16 years old—a wise youth group leader taught me that the best kind of time to give to God was the first time of my day. Like I wrote above, to wake up in prayer and be a "Yes!" girl to God's plans is the very beginning. To then focus on God in prayer and reading His Bible is the next, wise choice to make. After *all* these years, that is still how I spend the time right after my breakfast—and sometimes before!—reading the Bible and praying for the Holy Spirit to teach me through that precious Word.

God also challenged me, when a teenager, to spend other quiet times praying, worshiping Him, and studying His Word. Even on a Friday night in college, when all the other girls were going out on dates or going to the mall in a group, sometimes the "still, small voice" of God would lead me to just stay in my dorm and have a "date" with Jesus. You know what? Those were always very special times. In fact, it was on one of those special "date nights" with Jesus that He led me to read and study the Book of Ruth and taught me many of the things I have taught other girls and ladies for 40 years now!

> *Even on a Friday night in college, when all the other girls were going out on dates or going to the mall in a group, sometimes the "still, small voice" of God would lead me to just stay in my dorm and have a "date" with Jesus.*

The fact is that I have never outgrown those special dates. Have you ever been on a date with Jesus? Let me tell you about one of those times. Several years ago, I realized that I had a totally free Friday night (all my family was out of town). I asked myself, "What are you going to do with your free night?"

As soon as I asked myself that question, my heart's reply was, "I can go on a date with Jesus!" So I drove out to the beach where our family has a condo and spent the evening sitting on a balcony, eight floors up, waiting for the full moon to rise and enjoying a date with Jesus.

I brought along my Bible and journal and my prayer list. Just as I began to pray through some of the many prayer requests, I paused to look at the ocean, and suddenly I saw a rainbow. Now, a rainbow is not unique when it has rained—but it hadn't rained! I just gazed at that rainbow in awe and began to cry. Here I was, just beginning my date with Jesus, and He blessed me with a rainbow before the full moon came up. Talk about a double portion of blessing!

I started to think about what a rainbow means in the Bible—the faithful promise of the Lord—and I just cried, thinking of the many promises that God has made and *kept*. I decided to look up all the times in the Bible that rainbows are mentioned, and I discovered three men (Noah, Ezekiel, and John) who saw rainbows. Each of the rainbows was different, yet all three men had something in common—they each faced hard circumstances, difficult things happening in their lives. (See Genesis 9; Ezekiel 1; Revelation 4 and 10.)

As I thought about the rainbows that Ezekiel and John saw, I realized that they were being given visions that had to do with heaven. Heaven, our eternal home with God, is our greatest hope as believers in Jesus, and the rainbows that these men gazed upon were not simply scientific wonders, they were a vision of something that exists in heaven itself! I will never see a rainbow again without thinking about the rainbow that surrounds the throne of heaven (see Revelation 4:3) and heaven's rainbow of glory all around the Holy One (see Ezekiel 1:28).

On that high perch, with the bright moon lighting the beach, I thought about the gift God had given me that evening. What is it to experience the beauty of a rainbow *without going through a storm?* Here is what God showed me: *We can be rainbows of hope in people's lives even when they aren't facing storms.* Then, when their storms arrive—and they surely will—they will start looking for the rainbows of promise that speak to their hearts.

I raised my hands to praise the Lord for the insight about rainbows, and suddenly that enormous, full moon caught my eye again. It was so bright! I was captivated by it—do you know what it is to be "captivated"? It's like the very beauty of a thing takes you captive as you stare and actually feel how amazing it is. I was thinking about how very far away the moon was and about the great effort, focus, commitment, passion, money, and sacrifices used to land men on the moon and plant an American flag there more than 40 years ago. As I thought on this, my heart began to get sad, actually, as I realized that men could pay such a *huge price to touch the moon* but were rarely willing to act with such passion to touch the heart of the One who *made* the moon.

> *When I consider your heavens, the work of your fingers, the moon and the stars, which you have set in place, what is mankind that you are mindful of them…* (Psalm 8:3-4 NIV).

Driving back home from my date with Jesus, I opened my car's "full moon" roof and worshiped the Lord while that bright moon shone down on me! What an amazing return I got on the investment of that one Friday night. With faith, I gave God my time, and in return, the Lord gave me a rainbow and showed me a new truth about bringing hope and beauty into other people's lives. He gave me a radiant, shining moon and reminded me how I always want to help people seek Him, the creator of that stunning moon. This was what I call an evening of abundance! God met me on that balcony with a display of His splendor and ministry to my heart. Surrendering my "free" time to the Lord, my date with Jesus blessed me more than any trip to the mall or night with Netflix. His promise once again came true, *"Seek, and you will find"* (Matthew 7:7).

When I raised my right hand through the roof in praise, I started to grin, realizing that at that moment my raised hand touched the heart of the One who gave me a rainbow while I was waiting for a full moon. These are the kinds of precious gifts God gives to our hearts when we surrender totally to Him. Gifts of beauty, gifts of understanding, gifts of encouragement and joy. As you seek to be a Young Lady of Total Surrender, I pray that you will see more and more the gifts God gives you in return for breaking your alabaster box at His feet.

Discussion Questions

Here are some questions you can think about or write about or talk about with someone else. It's not a test! So, feel free to look back in the chapter to help you think about your answers.

1. How is the Bible character, Ruth, an example of total surrender? Can you list a few ways that Ruth shows *total surrender* through how she lived and the choices she made?

2. What does it look like to "Shout Yes" to God in your everyday life?

3. What is on the "other side" to saying *Yes* to God? In other words, what can happen in your life (and the lives of those around you) when you say "Yes" to God? [Think of examples like Mary or Ruth and how their "Yes" to God changed history!] Luke 1:37, 38

4. When the woman breaks the Alabaster Box over Jesus' feet, what is she saying to Him? (see Mark 14:3-9)

5. Why is it so important to trust your dreams, hopes and desires to Jesus?

6. Describe what a "date with Jesus" might look like to you.

Chapter 2

Becoming a Young Lady of Diligence

The Young Lady of Diligence can have a ministry of encouragement—to give someone who is discouraged a reason to keep going. –JMK

Ruth's Diligence

In each of this book's chapters, I'll be sharing with you more of the story of the Book of Ruth, and you'll see how the different heart attitudes show up. Let's pick up where Ruth has gone with Naomi to Israel and they are now getting settled in their new life there.

Understanding that God promised to provide for widows, Naomi sent Ruth to gather grain in the field of a relative, or, as the Bible says, a "kinsman." Ruth didn't complain about going to a barley harvest and picking up the leftovers that the poor were welcome to. She did not complain about walking into a field of strangers and starting such sweaty and hard work. Ruth was willing to work *diligently* at whatever her Lord called her to do. She was willing to work hard, which is what "diligent" means, and was even enthusiastic about going to the fields. The Bible says:

> *And Ruth the Moabitess said to Naomi, "Please let me go to the field and glean among the ears of grain after one in whose sight I may find favor." And she said to her, "Go, my daughter"* (Ruth 2:2).

When she and Naomi moved back to Bethlehem, Ruth did not waste a moment feeling sorry for herself. She went right to work. Instead of being saddened or frustrated by her situation of being a stranger in a new land, without the hope of marriage, she took advantage of the opportunities given her and diligently embraced each day.

Can you imagine what that might have been like for Ruth? Remember, she lost her husband, moved away from her homeland, and has now come to a foreign country where people did not favor her. I can only imagine that she must have felt lonely and even scared. *Yet*, the Word tells us that she put one foot in front of the other and stood by her choice to follow Naomi and serve Naomi's God. At this point in the story, this meant the humbling work of gathering the leftover grain on the edges of the field for the survival of her mother-in-law and herself.

And it's at this point in the story, when we see Ruth in those barley fields, that we meet the "leading man" in the love story of the Book of Ruth. It is here that we are introduced to Boaz. Now, Boaz was what we might call a rich "bachelor." He was not married. But as we will come to see, God had other plans for his future! Boaz paid attention to the young Moabite woman, Ruth, and the Bible explains to us that one of the reasons he was attracted to Ruth was her diligence while working in his field. Ruth was not afraid of hard work, and more than that, she was willing to work hard for the benefit of another person!

Boaz took notice of this very thing: that Ruth was working hard for her widowed mother-in-law Naomi, and not just for herself. *This* is an incredibly important quality to think about. So let's do just that. Many young people are willing to work hard for something they have their eye on—expensive jeans, a trendy purse, or some kind of phone. But honestly, working hard to help someone else might be rare in the lives of young people who don't "need" to work to care for a family or survive themselves. The fact that the Lord shows us that diligent work is valuable in His sight is certainly what makes me want to learn to be more like that! To help others with an attitude of love is a very high "call" in God's Word. This is why this part of Ruth's character is highlighted in the story. By describing how Boaz—an honorable man— sees her, we are being shown what is important to God. I *love* how God shows us through stories things that are important to Him, because there is nothing I want more in life that to learn more and more about what's important to my Father God!

In the rest of this chapter, I want to encourage you to see different areas where you can practice being a girl who is growing in diligence. And girls, diligence is not only "hard" work, it is also the willingness to press on when things are tough. It is also the mindset that focuses on a goal to help us do what we are trying to do. So, in learning about diligence, it is a *must* that we ask the Lord to help us see the goals He has for us. If Mom asks you to empty the dishwasher or to dust, the simple goal is for the house to get cleaned, but the *bigger* goals for you at that moment is to help your parent, to obey out of love and respect, and to show that you are part of the family "team" in making life run well. The *biggest* goal—and we all need help from the Holy Spirit to pay attention to this—is to learn about serving God.

You might think, "*How* on earth does *dusting* serve God?!" Well, if you learn to dust with a cheerful heart, thanking God for the home you have and that you are able to walk around, to use your hands and arms, to see and touch the cloth and the wood and the plastic…if you learn about setting your mind and heart in a good place while *dusting*, you are being trained to practice helpful, loving attitudes in all that you do. Just like we talked about steps on a journey in the Introduction, these are the steps that teach your heart and mind that you can choose to be grateful in simple things, that you can find joy in the smallest, everyday

*In learning about diligence, it is a **must** that we ask the Lord to help us see the goals He has for us.*

moments, and that you will be blessed and be a blessing in that process. Trust me when I tell you, to learn these things at your age will help you greatly through your whole life!

What It Takes to Be a World-Changer

Ruth's diligence was shown through her willingness to do what was required even when it did not seem to be a dream opportunity. Diligence strengthens a person with the ability to keep going long after everyone else has quit, either because the task was too hard or because it felt boring.

Have you seen people who are not willing to help out or to do what they are asked because they think it's not cool or they think it's "stupid" or boring? Sadly, I have seen plenty of this attitude—among young people and older ones. I have come to call this dangerous mindset an attitude of "care-less-ness," as in, "I couldn't care less!"

There was a wonderful book that came out a few years ago called *Kisses from Katie* about a girl, not too much older than you, who went to Africa to help orphans. Katie is an example of the opposite of care-less-ness. She, like Ruth, made some big choices to go where she felt God was calling her to go—even when other people thought she was insane! She pays close attention to people and she has seen that a lot of *small* choices add up to the kinds of things that can change lives—and even change the world! Here is what Katie said:

> People who really want to make a difference in the world usually do it, in one way or another. And I've noticed something about people who make a difference in the world: They hold the unshakable conviction that individuals are extremely important, that *every life matters*. They get excited over one smile. They are willing to feed one stomach, educate one mind, and treat one wound. They aren't determined to revolutionize the world all at once; they're satisfied with small changes. Over time, though, the small changes add up. Sometimes they even transform cities and nations, and yes, the world.[1]

Becoming a Young Lady of Diligence happens one small change at a time, not all at once! And sometimes it happens from the outside in. Sometimes we have to *do* the thing to *become* the thing. Doing kind things turns us into kind people. Doing generous things creates generous people.

These small changes will allow you to grow a "holy habit" of serving that will shape you into a world-changer. The activities I will share with you in the rest of this chapter are not difficult, and you can do them until serving becomes more and more just normal to you. It is a long list, I know, but read what you can each day for a few days and ask God to help you think about these different actions and

These small changes will allow you to grow a "holy habit" of serving that will shape you into a world-changer.

attitudes. You might find that it helps you to write them in your journal and to keep praying for God to show you how to get better at these things He calls *all* of us to do—I am still learning to grow in these areas! Every time you do something for someone other than yourself, you are becoming a Young Lady of Diligence.

Prayer

Diligence and "Internal Jogging"

Let's take some time to think about prayer. Maybe you have never thought about it like this, but prayer is a form of serving—maybe the most important form. To pray is to *pay attention* to our relationship with God. Sometimes we are praising God in prayer; sometimes we are asking Him to help us or others in our life. A *very* important part of prayer is learning to "listen" to the Holy Spirit. To pray is to say to God, "I need You for everything in my life! From my heartbeat and my breath, to my food and my friends, to my attitude and my choices." And the Lord *wants* us to admit that we need Him. He *wants* us to know how we are connected to Him as our Creator. When we know how totally dependent we are on God, how much we need Him, we learn that there is nothing too small to pray to our heavenly Father about and nothing too small to praise Him for—and this *blesses God!* When we know how much we need God, we get to learn how much He loves us!

Now, if you are anything like me, you have had to learn that most holy habits do *not* just come naturally and that praying takes "discipline." In other words, we need to choose to pray and make it high on our list each day. In fact, it has not been unusual for me to pray, "Oh, Papa God! Please help me to settle down and pray!" Not only do we need to decide to pray, we need to learn from older and wiser Christians about different ways to pray. Some days I sit down with my Bible and open it to a Psalm and pray about the things the Psalmist writes. Where Psalm 23 says, "The Lord is my Shepherd," I pray, "Thank You, Father God, for being my shepherd who cares for me and watches over me!" Then it says, "I do not lack," and I might pray, "Oh God, thank You that my family has enough food today," or "Jesus, will You please help me to *know* that I do not lack even if I feel lonely today?" You see? We can pray by following along with what God's Word says and by asking Him to help us understand it or see His truths in our lives.

As you learn about prayer, here's an area that's really important—*listening* to God. Some of you may know what this is like, others may not. And I want you to know that it can be different for different people at different times—and it is always an area to grow in! When we read God's Word we can "hear" the voice of God, because God wrote His Word through the people He chose to write the books of the Bible. That's why it's one of the best things in my life to read the Bible and memorize Bible verses—and why I spend so much of my time teaching and writing like a cheerleader for people to do the same! When I have felt lonely, like when no one remembered a special day, and a verse pops into my head, like Jeremiah 31:3, *"I have loved you with an everlasting love,"* it is the Spirit of the Lord reminding me that the *God of the whole universe loves me!* How awesome is *that?* Then I can respond by thanking God and also asking Him to help me know this great truth deep in my heart so that I am not so let down by other people *and* so that I can tell others how dearly *they* are loved by God.

Listening to God is described in the Bible as a *"still small voice"* (1 Kings 19:12 NKJV), which may not sound like someone talking into our ears, really, but more like a "nudge" that reminds us of a truth of God from His Word. Or maybe the nudge reminds us what a godly attitude of love and kindness, patience and generosity would be in the situation we are praying about. To listen to God often means that we ask Him to help our minds be quiet so that a hundred thoughts are not racing through our heads. In the Book of Isaiah, the prophet writes, *"In quietness and trust is your strength"* (Isaiah 30:15).

I once heard someone describe prayer as "internal jogging." You know what jogging is—it's running for exercise. So, prayer is like jogging in your heart and mind, jogging on the inside. For those of us who have jogged or who do dance or gymnastics (or in my life, I have done years of speed walking), we know that to get better and better at it takes time. Our muscles need to get stronger and more flexible to improve. You are never too young to learn how to "jog internally." The prayer life of a Young Lady of Diligence can have positive effects from a very young age. And, as with exercise, the only way to fail at prayer is to fail to show up at all! So, please remember, there is no such thing as a bad prayer or a lame prayer…the only bad thing is *no* prayer!

Prayer is like talking between two people who love each other. From a very early age (4 years old) I taught our daughter Jessi that she could pray about everything. As a young girl she learned to take notice of God in her everyday life, to be thankful and grateful for faith and for kindness, and to confess when her heart or her words got off track. As a tween and then a teen, she knew that when she was hurt or confused or angered in life, these were the perfect things to tell God in prayer—mean girls, sometimes even mean teachers, annoying boys, fights with BFFs, fears, hoped-for dreams, broken dreams, family difficulties, and other things that made her the most anxious or sad.

*There is no such thing as a bad prayer or a lame prayer...the only bad thing is **no** prayer!*

How often should you pray? The Bible tells us how often we should pray: *"Pray without ceasing"* (1 Thessalonians 5:17). Wow! This is telling us that our goal is to learn to pray about everything at any time! As I wrote before, you are never too young to learn that we need the Lord in *all* things.

Here is an example of something I wonder if you have thought about before. More than ever, it seems, we hear terrible stories about bullies at school or after school. When I teach a big group, lots and lots of girls and their moms have come to me with questions about the problems with "mean girls" at school. The first question I have for them is: "How often do you pray for these mean girls?"

Now, praying does not mean that you and your parents should not talk to the school's leaders; it does mean, though, that prayer is the *ultimate power* to handle not only mean girls but also every other annoying or hurtful person who will cross your paths. Think about it this way: If you could choose between a boy in your class or a superhero like *Thor* to fight an evil power, wouldn't you choose Thor? Praying and learning to wait on God is like asking Thor for help—but way better! It's not just a greater power, it's the ultimate power! In our home, whenever someone needed to talk about a difficult person, we always said, "Okay, what do we do about a difficult teacher or fellow student?" And the answer was always the same—"Pray for them! Overcome evil with good!"

> *Do not be overcome by evil, but overcome evil with good* (Romans 12:21).

A "Holy Hit List"

Mean or troublesome or hurtful people are very important to pray for. And here is another group of people to be praying for—other boys and girls who do not yet know that Jesus is their Savior. My advice is that people keep a list of these people right in the front of their Bible or journal, and I call this my "holy hit list." These are people I ask Jesus to hit "smack upside the head" with the *truth* of His love for them! You know why this kind of list is especially important to me and why I know it works? Because *I* came to know Jesus through being on the holy "hit lists" of several teens. They were in a weekly Bible study and were encouraged to write the names of the top ten kids at their school who they would love to see come to Jesus. *I was one of those kids.* Talk about a young person being a world-changer through prayer! That group of teens who prayed for me weekly changed my life for eternity. I was a lost girl from a very troubled home, and God used *other teenagers* to pray me into His Kingdom. Well, believe me, God can use the prayers of girls who are not even teenagers to do the same miracle!

When you make a list like this and pray for the kids on it, God will most likely use *you* in some way to be a witness to those kids you are praying for. Praying for me week after week gave these teens the courage to ask me—week after week—to come to their youth meeting. Their *diligence* in prayer allowed them to never give up on me, even after I said no to their invitations at least ten times!

Learning to pray for those who need Jesus is a *most* holy habit. We all have friends and relatives who need Jesus, and it is never too early to start praying for the salvation of relatives, neighbors, and kids or teachers at school.

Diligent Prayer about Your "Crushes"

The next kind of prayer I want to cheer you on to do may not seem needed yet for all of you, but some of you are old enough to have a "crush" on a boy, and the rest of you will in the coming years. Does it sound strange to you to pray about such a boy? Let's think about this: Why *don't* we pray about the boys we like? Girls and boys are naturally attracted to one another—it's how God has made people. So, because we know that's going to happen, the most important safeguard for a girl's heart is to guard her heart through prayer. Remember when I wrote about the signs that *guide* our hearts and *guard* our hearts? Well, praying about a boy you think is special or who makes your heart jump a little is like obeying a *stop sign* when driving. You need to *stop* and tell the Lord that you are thinking about this boy and his attention to you. *Stop* and tell God how you feel when you see this boy or talk with him. When you begin to wonder if he likes you or if he will ask you to hang out with him, *stop* and pray for *him!* Pray that the Lord will help him to make the best choices and for him to seek God in his life. It's so good to tell God what's going on in your mind *and* to tell a trusted person, be it your mom or your best friend, especially if your BFF is a girl who will pray for you!

> *Above all else, guard your heart, for everything you do flows from it* (Proverbs 4:23 NIV).

So, girls, remember, prayer is not only how to get ready for a great work, it *is* the greatest work. Think about this:

Daniel, one of the great prophets in the Bible, was taken captive to Babylon when he was just a teenager; but long before he was sent off to that foreign land, his parents taught him how to pray three times a day!

> *Three times a day he got down on his knees and prayed, giving thanks to his God, just as he had done before* (Daniel 6:10 NIV).

Becoming diligent pray-ers builds a strong base for all else a Young Lady of Diligence would seek to do.

Service

Diligence and Holy Sweat

My husband, Ken, that wonderful man who proposed to me at Cinderella's Castle, worked for 20 years in short-term missions. The name for the team of people who worked "behind the scenes" on their trips was the *Holy Sweat Team.* The teens on these teams got up before anyone else to make breakfast, and stayed longer after meals to clean up. The Holy Sweat Team often missed out on some of the fun free time and other activities.

Would you *want* to be on such a behind-the-scenes team? Why would someone do this?

Let's pull back from the scene of a mission trip and take a look at how you serve on your home turf. Are you willing to clear the kitchen table without being asked? Does it take

Mom pushing you to have you put dishes in the dishwasher? Some young people act like helping around the house is a punishment; but you can learn another way of thinking about helping at home (or school or church) as a *blessing to others* and not a curse. In fact, working up a holy sweat of service is an offering to God—a "sweat offering" that will come back as a blessing upon your own heart.

The same thing is true at church. Have you been willing to help out with a ministry at church, like serving in the nursery, Vacation Bible School for younger kids, or maybe an all-church work day? The more you are willing to serve, the more likely your heart will grow in an attitude of diligence. There is such a blessing in serving others.

> ...*Whoever refreshes others will be refreshed* (Proverbs 11:25 NIV).

A P-31 Woman in Training

Becoming a Young Lady of Diligence is really a P-31 Woman in training. What on earth is a P-31 Woman? Well, P-31 is short for Proverbs 31, the very last chapter in the Book of Proverbs. Here is a great activity: Read Proverbs 31:10-31 and highlight the things that the P-31 Woman does and what her attitudes are to do those things. When we look at the projects the P-31 Woman was doing, we know

Working up a holy sweat of service is an offering to God—a "sweat offering" that will come back as a blessing upon your own heart.

that she didn't just learn these activities after she got married. We can be sure that the P-31 Woman was in training as a Young Lady of Diligence long before that!

> *She selects wool and flax and works with eager hands. She sets about her work vigorously; her arms are strong for her tasks* (Proverbs 31:13,17 NIV).

Do you know the word *vigorous*? It means to be strong and eager, and it comes from the word *vigor*. Do you know how the P-31 Woman became vigorous? The strength and vigor of a P-31 Woman began when she was a little girl, the first time she helped load the dishwasher or pick up the toys or helped cook a meal. Every time you clean up your room or help bring in the groceries, you are developing muscles for being a strong, smart P-31 Woman someday. Every time you volunteer at church or school, you are building strength to be a giving person. When your friends ask you why you are volunteering, you can tell them you are a P-31 Woman in training! And guess what kind of husband a P-31 Woman attracts? She will be the kind of young woman who gets the attention of a "prince of a guy"—like Boaz! A Bozo guy is too selfish to notice anything honorable!

Generosity

Diligence and Breaking One's Piggy Bank

Another area where you can become a Young Lady of Diligence is in giving money unselfishly for the needs of others—what is also called generosity. It touches my heart when I see a young person give to a needy cause—whether in church, school, or community. Most girls don't have very much money, but to give away some of that money to be used for needy people is an action that shines with the love of Jesus.

When our daughter was in third grade, her class put together a care package for a missionary family in Japan. She came home and asked if we could go to the store and buy banana Nerds and red licorice for the missionary children. I may have laughed right out loud with delight, imagining these children finding those treats in their packages—and even sharing them with their little Japanese friends. As an eight-year-old, Jessi's heart wanted to reach out and bless the children of the missionaries—and what better way than with her favorite candy!

When our son was in seventh grade, he had saved a pretty large sum of money that he wanted to spend on a special trip we would be taking during Christmas vacation. As the trip drew near, Ben found out about a need of his favorite teacher. He came home from school and told my husband and me that he wanted to give this teacher all the money he had saved, so the teacher could fix his broken car. We were so blessed by this godly desire that we actually were in tears as we told him how noble his choice was.

Girls and boys have such tender hearts. The P-31 Woman would surely have learned giving as a child, because the

Word tells us about her generous giving as an adult. Proverbs 31:20 explains: *"She opens her arms to the poor and extends her hands to the needy"* (NIV).

Encouragement

Maddie and Libby's Story

There is a word that I have used many times already in this book that I am sure you know—I sure hope you do! That word is *encourage*, and if you break it up, you can see that it's en-courage, which means "to fill someone with courage." There are other ways of understanding this idea, but that's a great image—to give someone courage, to help them when they feel weak or afraid or tired. The Bible tells us that encouragement is a gift. God gives some people the ability to be especially encouraging, but indeed, we are all called to encourage one another.

How old does a girl have to be to encourage another girl spiritually? Some people think a girl has to be in high school to encourage a struggling best friend. Yet here's great news—there is no age limit on God using a young heart. There is no minimum weight or height for the love of God to pour through the heart of a girl.

A grandmother I know tells a wonderful story of a late-night talk between two BFFs that she overheard. These girls were not seniors in high school; they were in elementary school—they may have been even younger than you! One night Maddie, who was ten years old, couldn't get to sleep, because she was so nervous and sad that her family was moving, taking her away from other family and friends. Unable to sleep, Maddie texted her friend Libby and told her how anxious she was about moving. Libby texted back and told her friend to read from the Book of James, chapter 1:1-8, three times to help her heart calm down.

When I heard this story, tears filled my eyes, and joy filled my heart, because I know that God can use any heart that is growing in Jesus. Libby, at the age of 11, had already been learning how to encourage her friend toward trusting God instead of letting sadness and nervousness overtake her.

> *And let us consider how we may spur one another on toward love and good deeds* (Hebrews 10:24 NIV).

In three of the Gospels we are told how Jesus encouraged the people to allow the children to come to Him (see Matthew 19:14; Mark 10:14; Luke 18:16). He knew that children are open and teachable. Jesus showed the adults he was talking to that children can be used by God. Don't think that age has anything to do with whether God can use you to bless and encourage others! Even a girl much younger than you can learn to love and be kind and to serve God—like the priest in the Bible, Samuel, who served in the Temple beginning at the age of kindergarten!

Diligence and "Fresh Air"

Libby helped Maddie by "spurring her on" to read and be comforted by God's Word that night. We can be sure that as

BFFs, they encouraged each other in lots of ways. Here is one of my favorite ways to send a little courage to people—write them a kind note. From a young age I have known the power of the written word to be like fresh air to another soul.

There are so many ways to send someone words, be it a card that you make or buy or a letter, e-mails, or texting. I still am thrilled when I get a card or a letter in the mailbox, especially because we don't send as many things through the mail as we used to. It doesn't have to be a birthday for you to send a card or write a thoughtful e-mail to a friend or family member who is having a hard day—or a hard month! Like Libby, you can share a Bible verse that brings hope right from God's Word to a sad or lonely heart. The prophet Isaiah wrote out the perfect formula for this world-changing ministry of encouragement:

> *The Master, God, has given me a well-taught tongue, so I know how to encourage tired people.*
>
> *He wakes me up in the morning, wakes me up, opens my ears to listen as one ready to take orders.*
>
> *The Master, God, opened my ears, and I didn't go back to sleep, didn't pull the covers back over my head* (Isaiah 50:4-5 MSG).

Do you notice something familiar sounding in that Bible verse? It sounds to me like Isaiah is describing a "shout *Yes*!" way to wake up. And remember earlier in this chapter when

I wrote about listening to God? He's talking about that, too, isn't he? What is the "well-taught tongue" he writes about? I bet you know. It's how we know to speak—or write—when we have spent time learning God's Word. The well-taught tongue can share the kind of words that help lead a person's attention to the hope of God's many promises.

So, whether e-mailing, texting, or even writing a card, God's girls can keep hope alive in the hearts of those they love—simply by being cheerleaders of truth!

Hospitality

Diligence and a Junk-Food Drawer

The next holy habit you can develop is *hospitality.* If you have heard this term in your own home, you know it has to do with being welcoming and generously having people come to eat or even stay overnight. Hospitality is learned with the simplest offering to a visiting friend of a snack or a bottle of cold water.

In our kitchen we had a "junk-food drawer" (what I called it), or a "treat drawer" (what the kids called it). I have to laugh, because even though I know that a lot of sweets are not good for me, I still like a treat sometimes! But I still called it a junk-food drawer. Our children knew they could always offer their friends something from this drawer. In fact, it was the one drawer that was broken in our kitchen, because it was used so much. Though our home was not very large, our children always felt free to invite their friends to come over. Part of *their* hospitability habit was to invite their friends or cousins to feel free to take a treat from the junk-food drawer.

Hospitality may seem so simple, but there are reasons it is given such importance in the Bible. Without a doubt it is a little act of kindness that allows for big returns: people feeling loved and cared for and paid attention to.

We love God best when we love each other well.

Diligence and Holy Hugs

Finally, here's another holy habit that is even more simple than hospitality. A good hug is a gift to the human heart. To give an encouraging hug, you don't need special training, a college degree, or a bank account. Yet the good that comes from it is priceless.

Do you greet others with a holy hug? Are you comfortable hugging someone who is crying or upset? This gift to the heart means that we need to be others-centered, thinking about what would comfort someone, especially for those of us who are not "natural" huggers.

Now, I know that not everyone is the hugging type. But I am going to encourage everyone I can to *learn* to be the hugging type. I am so sure that God is all about hugging!

Do you know where I get that from? There is a verse that describes those whom God loves as "resting between His shoulders." Sounds like a holy hug to me!

> *Let the beloved of the Lord rest secure in him, for he shields him all day long, and the one the Lord loves rests between his shoulders* (Deuteronomy 33:12 NIV).

Many years ago, two teenage girls knocked on my door. When I opened the door, I recognized one of my daughter's friends (let's pretend her name is Kelsey), and the other girl was a stranger. I welcomed them both and offered them something to drink. When Kelsey introduced the other girl to me, I heard the name and remembered that this girl had gotten in a lot of trouble at school. She was a girl who was not too popular with other girls. Kelsey said, "Mrs. Kendall, I told my friend here that you wrote a book and that you might give her a copy."

I happily jumped up and got her a copy and signed it to her. When the two girls got ready to leave, of course I gave them both big hugs, and I noticed that this girl, who I had never met before that day, held on to me for a few moments longer with an extra tight squeeze.

That night Kelsey called and said, "Mrs. Kendall, the minute we got in the car my friend said, 'I don't remember the last time an adult hugged me!'" Wow. I was both sad for that girl and humbled that God had used my "holy habit" of hugging to touch her heart and bless her.

It was a simple hug, but what that means to someone, only Jesus knows. He alone, who has touched the feelings of our hearts' hurts (see Hebrews 4:15), knows how deeply this girl's heart was touched. Later I heard that this troubled girl loved my book. My heart's cry was, "Lord Jesus, forgive us for judging troubled teens rather than praying for their hurting souls to be healed!"

Hurting souls lead so many teen girls to making poor and harmful choices!

A holy hug, some encouraging words, an open heart and home, a willingness to serve, and a heart bent toward our Lord in prayer—these are the kinds of exercises to practice as you are becoming a Young Lady of Diligence. In the next chapter, we will dive deeper into what will help you grow in diligence as we look at the power of faith.

Note

1. Katie Davis, *Kisses from Katie: A Story of Relentless Love and Redemption* (New York: Simon & Schuster, Inc, 2011), xi.

Discussion Questions

Here are some questions you can think about or write about or talk about with someone else. It's not a test! So, feel free to look back in the chapter to help you think about your answers.

1. Based on Ruth's story, explain how Ruth was diligent. What does diligence look like to you?
2. How can being diligent—working hard and enthusiastically—actually lead you into places where you experience blessing and opportunity? [like Ruth meeting Boaz] Heb. 11:6
3. How did Ruth catch Boaz's attention?
4. What does *being diligent* look like in your world?
5. Explain how obeying your parents, doing chores and serving other people actually *serves God*?

    Now, I want you to write out the *blessing* and *benefits* that your diligence brings. How do you get blessed by obeying your parents? How is your family blessed when you do chores? How are other people blessed when you volunteer your time to serve them? It's very important that you get a clear picture of how *your diligence* brings blessing into your life, and even more so, the lives of other people.

6. *Spiritual Diligence.* How does being diligent in the following areas bring blessing—to you and to others:

    a. Praying over a "Holy Hit List"

    b. Specifically praying for the guys you like

    c. Serving other people ("Holy Sweat")

    d. Being generous

    e. Giving encouragement

    f. Holy Hugs

    g. Hospitality

Chapter 3

Becoming a Young Lady of Faith

Faith in God and His ways and His timing is the most important heart guard there is. –JMK

Ruth's Faith

As you know, the Book of Ruth is named after its leading lady. This leading lady had a heart of faith that you have already learned about in the very beginning of the story. When Ruth left her hometown security for a new home with Naomi, that was an act of true faith. In fact, that one choice would lead her into a life that would need *daily* faith by Ruth. It was her faith that led her to say *no* to the gods of her childhood and *yes* to the one true God.

> *But Ruth said, "Do not urge me to leave you or turn back from following you; for where you go, I will go, and where you lodge, I will lodge. Your people shall be my people, and your God, my God"* (Ruth 1:16).

In the next part of the story, this faith-choice led Ruth to be obedient to her mother-in-law and go the field where she would meet her prince and quickly enter her "happily ever after." Ruth chose to trust God with her future. She looked not with the sight of her actual eyes, but through what we call "the eyes of faith." What her mind could not yet understand, she trusted God for. She believed with her heart for *His* version of her future.

And so it was that God directed Ruth to the field of Boaz. You'll find this divine meeting in chapter 2 of the Book of Ruth. It began when *"...she happened to come to the portion of the field belonging to Boaz..."* (Ruth 2:3). Ruth's eyes of faith led her to the exact spot where she would meet Mr. Right—Boaz. And here's something that's so cool! The name "Boaz" in Hebrew means "a pillar of strength." So, God rewarded Ruth's faith with a husband who lived up to his name.

In your walk of faith, I want to encourage you in *very practical* ways of building your faith. How do we grow in faith? The Bible is filled with teaching about this process; and so it is from God's Word that we find instruction in becoming a Young Lady of Faith. As Paul wrote to the Roman Church in his awesome letter encouraging them:

> *So faith comes from hearing, and hearing by the word of Christ* (Romans 10:17).

Let me repeat what I wrote in Chapter 2 about listening to God. When we study the Bible, we "hear" God's love for us and His instruction to us; we hear about God's character and about the character He would grow in us. It is not just any word we are hearing, but the *Word of God* that inspires and feeds our faith. Therefore, the absolute best thing I can focus this chapter on is how you can set *your* focus on God's Word, the Bible.

Getting Your "Seven" Daily

Within just seconds of asking Jesus to come into my heart and take control of my life, when I was 16 years old, I was given my first Bible. Along with it, the youth leader gave me the most important advice I have ever had. He said, "Jackie, this is your spiritual food. I want you to read it at least seven minutes each day. Seven minutes reading your Bible will begin to feed your spirit."

As a not-so-sweet 16-year-old who had just received God's glorious gift of forgiveness, I was in a very teachable mode. I took the instruction to "get my seven" very seriously, and actually couldn't wait to read my Bible! From that day until this day, I have always known that being able to read the Bible is a privilege, and through it, I have been blessed in *countless* ways!

When we study the Bible, we "hear" God's love for us and His instruction to us; we hear about God's character and about the character He would grow in us.

A No-Bozo Heart Guard

When I explained in the Introduction that we would be hearing about two kinds of guys in this book, you probably remember that I named them Boaz and Bozo. You've already read some about Boaz and how he was a man who saw the honorable ways Ruth acted; so now, let's talk more about this "Bozo" kind of guy. A Bozo is a boy who might be very selfish or unkind—even mean. He doesn't care about other people and does things to get in trouble or to hurt others. We all have bad days or times when we struggle with sin, but a Bozo is someone who is selfish, mad, or thoughtless *a lot*. It's like these ways of acting are his favorite ways. And I want to remind you that it's very important to pray for a boy like this and to hope for him to know God and to grow a softer heart! However, the trouble girls can get into is thinking they can *change* a boy like this. Believe me, my young friends, I have watched girls and women for years and seen how foolish they can be when it comes to making friends with boys and men! I have seen *way* too many women get their hearts broken by connecting themselves to *Bozo* guys—so I am writing this book to *you* to teach you young how not to do that!

Do you know what it means to "guard your heart"? It's a term we get right from the Bible, where Proverbs 4:23 says, *"Above all else, guard your heart, for everything you do flows from it"* (NIV). To guard your heart is to protect your mind and emotions from being hurt *as well as* from hurting others. Now, if someone spends her day thinking "I hate that girl! She is such a loser and she just annoys me majorly!" do you think it would be easy to try and be nice to or make friends with the "hated" girl? Of course not. These kinds of thoughts being practiced and repeated all day long completely wear away any kindness someone could show to that girl. A different example would be if you found yourself interested in a boy who was mean to other people or who was jerk or a show-off in class. *Maybe* he was nicer to you than he was to other people, so you find yourself thinking thoughts like, "He is sooo cute. I just love how he makes me laugh. I am *so* lucky he talks to me at lunch more than any other girls." Would thoughts like that guide you closer to the boy or farther away from him? You know the answer: They would guide your heart to want *more* of his attention—even if you knew that he really was a Bozo.

So, girls, if there were *one thing* I could tell you about that would help *guard your hearts* and guide them in the right direction, it would be to "Get Your Seven!" Getting your seven in the Word is a great No-Bozo Heart Guard. Why do I believe that? When a girl gets (at least!) her seven minutes in God's Word every day, she can't help but grow spiritually. This growth then moves a desire in her to please the Lord, and it makes her *less attracted* to guys who are not growing in their love for the Lord as she is. This is not a magic formula; this is just an example of *the transforming power of God's Word in our hearts.*

I didn't have a Christian mother or father. I lived in a deeply disturbed home, where there was a lot of anger and hurt and even physical abuse. But my time in God's Word strengthened my heart and developed a No-Bozo Heart Guard in the middle of family and friends who were not following Jesus. The challenges I faced in life required a strong faith. And where does faith come from? Well, it is a gift from God, and therefore it is connected to one's daily "face time" *with God.* We sure didn't have iPhones when I was a teenager, but I could daily call God and have "face time" with Him, and I *know* that this was one of the most important things that helped me to avoid a Bozo in a husband!

Here's a quote my beloved college mentor shared with me almost 40 years ago. It is still true today:

> There is no success, no happiness, and no fulfillment in life apart from a consistent, daily, growing relationship with Jesus through the *Word.*[1]

"Consistent," as you might know, means that something is done by a regular pattern, again and again and again, every day. Hopefully you are consistent in brushing your teeth. You're certainly consistent about eating every day! Maybe you consistently talk to or text the same friend every day. If we know how to be consistent in things like that, we definitely have the ability to learn to be consistent in reading our Bibles and praying. Too many girls are passing school but flunking life, because they never learned the formula for success in life—*get your seven*. Now that you know it, *let's do it!*

Too Busy to "Get Your Seven"

Now, I know you're busy. Of course you are. If you're over six years old, you're busy in one way or another. Isn't it interesting, though, that we're never too busy to eat? We're never too busy to shop. Never too busy to text or tweet or pose for another selfie. We're never too busy, it seems, to watch our favorite shows. We constantly complain about the busyness in our lives…and say we are just too busy to spend time in God's Word.

This is shocking to me! Do you know why? Not because people aren't following *a rule* to have a quiet time. It's shocking because I have gotten *so much* comfort and encouragement and wisdom from the Father so regularly from His Word that *I can't imagine someone missing out on those blessings!* Not only that, but I don't want anyone to miss out! I want as many people as possible to know the joy and comfort and strength I have had from a living relationship with God—and this is exactly why I do what I do in writing and teaching. Right now as I type these words, I feel like I am grabbing your hand and saying, "Come with me, precious girl! Come see the awesome and amazing gifts God has for you in His Bible!"

So, if you think you are too busy to read the Bible, *I promise you*, you aren't. You can learn how to become a consistent Bible reader just like you learn how to do anything else—choice and practice. You choose it and then you practice it. And there are creative ways to do this! I have a friend who likes to blow her hair straight with a diffuser. This takes a bit more time in the morning, so this woman uses that time wisely. She opens her Bible, and as she is blowing her hair dry and straight, she is turning the pages, reading and praying.

Here is a great tool for you (LOL, no, not the diffuser!): Many of the women I am close to use the *One Year Bible* as their way to get their daily seven. I have also worked with professional baseball and football players who struggle to make time to read the Bible with all the work it takes to be a pro athlete, and this method has helped many of *them* be consistent, too.

You can learn how to become a consistent Bible reader just like you learn how to do anything else–choice and practice.

Why this Bible? Because the *One Year Bible* offers a daily format that helps us to be consistent. Every day's reading is divided into four parts—Old Testament, New Testament, Psalms, and Proverbs. These bite-sized morsels of Scripture help us to be nourished and to have spiritual energy throughout the day; and with four sections, there are four chances to get something meaningful out of our face time with God. Even if you can't buy a *One Year Bible* or you need to wait until Christmas or a birthday to ask for one, you can put bookmarks in your own Bible that remind you to read a few verses from each section of the Bible listed above.

Honestly, if you didn't learn anything from reading the Word, if you didn't see how God was encouraging you or guiding you in His ways, why would you read it? This does not mean that every day brings some deep or new understanding, but if you don't pay attention to God's Love Letter *daily*, you have less and less of a chance for His words and His ways of showing love to you to be clear to you.

I am blessed with a large group of friends, and we are all crazy busy. But we are also serious about keeping our friendships strong. That means that we choose to plan and make times to be with each other. What kinds of plans do you make to keep up a great relationship with your BFF? Do you plan special times to meet at school or after school? Do you ask your moms for sleepovers or for your friends to do things with you on the weekends? What if you didn't make plans on purpose? Maybe you would run into each other sometimes...but your friendship would weaken if you stopped calling, texting, and making arrangements to spend time together. You wouldn't know what each other was going through, what your hopes were, what each other's joys and troubles were. Making plans on purpose is what we call *intentional*—you know, like what you *intend* to do. Our goal is to be as *intentional* about our relationship with Jesus as we are with anyone else we most love. Hopefully your friends feel free to *help you* be intentional in your relationship with Him, as well.

One time a few years ago I was teaching at a mother-daughter event and I shared about this very thing I am writing to you—spending time each day reading the Bible. I suggested that the little girls (ages four through nine) go through the devotional *Lady in Waiting for Little Girls*, and I also reminded them that they could look up each verse in the devotional and mark it with a highlighter. Then they would not only have read the verses, but marked them in *their own* Bibles!

Two days later, a mother sent me the *sweetest picture*! It was a picture of her six-year-old daughter, Nancy Claire, who was in her pajamas, with her blanket and stuffed animal at her side—just the picture you would imagine of a little one snuggling up before bed. On her lap was an open Bible, and in her hand was a blue highlighter. I just cried when I saw the picture. I was so touched, because I knew that Nancy Claire was learning to practice a consistent, daily, growing relationship with Jesus and His Word.

Nancy Claire is learning at a young age that *sin will keep you from the Bible, but the Bible will keep you from sin.*

> *I have hidden your Word in my heart that I might not sin against You* (Psalm 119:11 NIV).

If you already have a consistent time in God's Word, then you can focus on encouraging your friends or your siblings to develop this holy habit. If, however, you have let your face time with God disappear from your daily schedule, then today is a great day to start again! Whether you need to encourage your BFF or you need the reminder yourself—or both—the following material will help you.

Hiding the Word in Your Heart

A fun way of Bible study is to read through the New Testament (for at least seven minutes each day), and draw a heart in the center of a journal page. Then, inside the heart, write the "address" of the verse that you really noticed that day. I like to say that something "jumped off the page" as I was reading. *In fact*, it is always best to pray before you begin reading, and ask the Lord to *show you* some idea or word that you can really learn from that day. Once you write where the words came from in the Bible *inside* the heart, you can write out the verse *under* the heart. This method has helped thousands of people to hide the Word of God in their own hearts!

A Quiet Time "KISS" Method for You

Most of us need a *simple* way to get our "seven" consistently. The Quiet Time KISS Method has worked for me and for many others I know. Do you know what K.I.S.S. stands for? It means, "Keep it Simple, Silly"! Sometimes we make things harder than they need to be, don't we?

I know a precious young woman named Courtney who made up a simple plan to encourage teen girls to consistently get their "seven." Here are Courtney's own words from an e-mail telling about what she calls the G.B.T.O—Girl Behind the Outfit:

> What can help you with staying consistent?—G.B.T.O....just as you lay your clothes out the night before school or your game...also lay out your devotional book and Bible where you are going to be reading the next day, with your clothes... this way you are not only making it easier to get into the Word (PREPARATION), but you are showing God that you are not only concerned with adorning your outward self, but also your HEART! (See 1 Peter 3:3-4.)

This is what I call intentional! The simple act of putting your Bible and journal out with your clothes means that you are *planning* to read your Bible in the morning. You are making a plan and setting your mind on becoming a more beautiful "girl behind the outfit." This is surely an act of faith that honors God!

Red Circle of Trust

My first college mentor, M.E. Cravens, taught me a way to strengthen my faith that I have shared with thousands. She encouraged me to buy a red pencil. What was the red pencil for? I was instructed to start reading through the Book of Psalms and use the red pencil to circle the word *trust* every time I saw it.

So, each day I would read a psalm and be on the hunt for another entry in the "Red Circle of Trust." M.E. Cravens knew that the most important thing she could teach me was to trust God more deeply. She also knew that to have such deep trust, you need deep faith, and faith was not something you buy at Target or Walmart. Faith develops through regular time in God's Word.

The simple activity of circling the word *trust* began the healing of a deep heart wound in me that was only visible to God and those closest to me.

Ruth and a Kidnapped Girl—Two Hearts of Faith

Now I will introduce you to another girl in the Bible whose faith is also inspiring. She, like Ruth, had a heart of faith that helped each of them in a new place, a new country, among new people.

Here is the second girl's story. She is one of my heroes. In the fifth chapter of the book Second Kings, we read about the healing of the leper, Naaman. Naaman was a famous army leader who had leprosy. He was finally healed by listening to the prophet Elisha and dipping himself in the Jordan River seven times.

> *So he went down and dipped himself seven times in the Jordan, according to the word of the man of God; and his flesh was restored like the flesh of a little child and he was clean* (2 Kings 5:14).

This is the miracle most people pay attention to when they read this story in the Bible. But there was actually another miracle told about in this story that is often missed by the untrained eye! Let's see if you can spot it:

> *Now Naaman, captain of the army of the king of Aram, was a great man with his master, and highly respected, because by him the Lord had given victory to Aram. The man was also a valiant warrior, but he was a leper. Now the Arameans had gone out in bands and had taken captive a little girl from the land of Israel; and she waited on Naaman's wife. She said to her mistress, "I wish that my master were with the prophet who is in Samaria! Then he would cure him of his leprosy." Naaman went in and told his master, saying, "Thus and thus spoke the girl who is from the land of Israel"* (2 Kings 5:1-4).

Did you catch the miracle? Did you see the miracle of a young Israelite girl who was kidnapped, taken to a foreign land, and made to be a servant? This girl was not bitter. Did she not miss her family and her hometown?

Was she not a victim of heartless kidnapping? *Yes, yes, yes!* But according to what the Scripture tells us about her, this young girl did not let bitterness define her. She did not hold on to unforgiveness like a kind of treasure. Rather, she stated her confidence in the healing God of Israel, and she boldly declared this to her mistress! Somehow this girl had been raised with such a confidence in God that even in cruel captivity, she could not hide her faith in God. In Hebrew, one of the many names used for our Lord God is "Jehovah-Rapha," which means "The Lord who Heals." This little girl had been taught that God was a God of healing—and she was brave enough to speak up and tell her captors about it!

My granddaughter's storybook Bible tells about this forgiving child's heart perfectly:

> Why would she, of all people, want to help Naaman? Didn't she hate him and want to hurt him back? Didn't she want to make him pay for the wrong he'd done? That is what you would expect, but instead of hating him, she loved him. Instead of hurting him back, she forgave him.

This little girl's parents not only taught her to depend on God and His truths, they also taught her how to love by forgiving even what would seem unforgivable.

There are many hard times that can come in our lives. A growing faith does not protect us from sadness or pain, but it will help us to make good choices in difficult situations—like this kidnapped little girl who did what was right. Even though she had every reason to withhold goodness from her mistress and master, she shared the hope of God's healing with a very sick man. Even though she faced a cruel exit from her parents and hometown, her parents did such a good job teaching her the truths of God's Word that she showed great faith and wisdom anyway.

Remember, faith comes by hearing and hearing by God's Word (see Romans 10:17). This young girl heard enough truth while she was growing up that it gave her strength even in captivity.

> *Obey them completely, and you will display your wisdom and intelligence among the surrounding nations* (Deuteronomy 4:6 NLT).

The Greatest Benefit of Bible Reading: A Growing Faith

A growing faith is a must. A growing faith will help you see who the Bozo guys are who don't love Jesus. It will help you pray for them but not attach yourself to them. A growing faith will support you when your BFF is not speaking to you or on those Friday nights when you are not allowed to go to the party where other kids are making poor choices.

A growing faith will help you when you can't date until you are 16. And even when you can date, a growing faith will give you *peace* when you find yourself without anyone to hang out with but Mom and Dad on yet another Friday night (my own daughter lived through this many, many times!).

A growing faith will encourage you when you feel like you have no friends. When you go to college or get a job and you are shocked that you are *still* not dating, a growing faith will hold you up. If you dream of being a wife and a mom, but it doesn't happen when you thought it might, this faith will steady your heart. This growing faith will give you patience to *wait on God* for a godly guy to befriend and date and eventually marry. Faith in God and His ways and His timing is the most important heart guard there is, whether you are 10 or 60!

There is so much more—everything in life—that faith guides us through and supports us in. Throughout 40 years of ministry, the story I hear over and over is of girls becoming shipwrecked in the storms of relationships. They are hit and almost sunk by what they expect in this part of their lives. So I want you to grow in faith *now* to keep your focus on the King of the Universe who loves you. Just because a girl is too young to date doesn't mean it's too early to train her heart toward the Lover of her soul.

Like our heroine Ruth, you can make a difference in this world through the daily growing of your faith in our precious God. Why don't you write the following verse on a sticky note and stick it on your bathroom mirror? Of all the verses in the Bible, it was *this* verse that I framed and gave to my friends as a party favor at a big birthday celebration! This verse will help you remember that God has plans for your life that He planned "long ago." In *Him* and *His plans*, we want to put our faith and hope!

> *Lord, you are my God; I will exalt you and praise your name, for in perfect faithfulness you have done wonderful things, things planned long ago* (Isaiah 25:1 NIV).

Note

1. One of my mentors, M.E. Cravens, made this statement in 1975. Also, see my book, *The Mentoring Mom* (Birmingham, AL: New Hope Publishers, 2006), 68.

Discussion Questions

Here are some questions you can think about or write about or talk about with someone else. It's not a test! So, feel free to look back in the chapter to help you think about your answers.

1. Write out some of the steps of faith that Ruth took in her journey. [It's important for you to see how faith takes action. Ruth didn't just *say* she had faith; she made life-changing choices that showed her faith]
2. How did Ruth's faith and trust in God actually lead her to the field where Boaz was?
3. What do you think it looks like to *build up your faith.* In other words, how can your faith grow and develop so that it gets stronger?
4. Think about some of the practical, everyday ways of building up your faith. One of the easiest is spending time in God's Word—the Bible.
   a. How can spending time reading the Bible strengthen your faith? [Rom. 10:17]
   b. What kind of relationship do you have with God's Word? If you are not spending daily time reading your Bible, I encourage you to start getting your *Daily Seven.* This is a simple way to start building up your faith.

5. What does it mean to "guard your heart?" How can spending time in the Bible help you guard your heart? [Proverbs 4:23]

6. How can your faith protect you from getting into bad relationships and keep you living passionately for God—even when you go through tough times?

Chapter 4

Becoming a Young Lady of Virtue

What we attract reveals our heart. –JMK

Ruth's Virtue

Let's talk about bling.

Ha! See, I got your attention there! But I'm really not kidding. I love jewelry. My dad was a master jeweler, and I watched him put together gorgeous pieces, setting diamonds and pearls in rings and brooches and necklaces. One of my favorite ways to "create" in my mind is to design jewelry—it's so much fun to imagine how the different components would go together. And here's an amazing thing about "bling": All that shining beauty comes out of extreme circumstances. Right? Gold is forged in a fire, diamonds and other precious gems are made from intense amounts of pressure under the weight of the earth, and pearls are actually the result of years and years of pain and irritation.

The pearl begins as a mere grain of sand in the belly of an oyster. But the annoying rubbing of that particle causes the oyster to produce layers and layers of a substance to protect itself from the agitation of the sand. A grain of sand, if you look at it under a microscope or see a magnified picture, looks something like a many-sided crystal with pointy corners and sharp edges. When this rubs up against the soft flesh of the oyster, it hurts! So God made that shelled creature with the ability to secrete a substance that covers all those sharp edges over and makes a very smooth and glossy treasure.

Like the oyster, Ruth went through many irritations and trials in her young life. She grieved the deaths of her father-in-law, brother-in-law, and husband. She bravely faced the chaos of a radically changed direction in her life as well as a move to a foreign land with a bitter mother-in-law. When she arrived in that strange land, the trials did not end. She was immediately thrown into a new working situation among total strangers with new customs. Through all this stress, her new faith began to wrap itself around the painful situations. The by-product was a beautiful pearl.

What was it that allowed Ruth to catch Boaz's attention? Was it her gorgeous hair or stunning eyes? No! The answer is found in Boaz's response to her question in Ruth, chapter 2.

Then she fell on her face, bowing to the ground and said to him, "Why have I found favor in your sight that

> *you should take notice of me, since I am a foreigner?" Boaz replied to her, "All that you have done for your mother-in-law after the death of your husband has been fully reported to me, and how you left your father and your mother and the land of your birth, and came to a people that you did not previously know"* (Ruth 2:10-11).

Boaz was attracted to the pearl of Ruth's virtue and character that he saw in her life. A woman of virtue is *so* attractive to a godly man. It is a pearl worth finding.

Virtue Attracts Virtue

Let's look at two words that are very important! They are *moral* and *virtue*. You may know these words, or you may have heard them, but let's review what they mean so that it's clear for the topic of this chapter. To be "moral" is to follow the best ways for good behavior. One can be moral in business by being honest with customers and fair to workers; you are moral in your schooling by following the rules for conduct in the classroom and on the playground, by not cheating on homework and by being honest and respectful of your teachers. When it comes to relationships between boys and girls (and later men and women), to be moral would mean to follow God's teachings about the right ways to express physical affection. If a young couple is dating or engaged to be married, God's Word is clear that the sexual relationship belongs to marriage. Guarding your own heart and body as a girl who is a long way from marriage is part of what it means for you to be moral.

The second word, *virtue*, really describes the first word. A Young Lady of Virtue is simply a young lady who sets her goal on being moral. In fact, one definition of virtue is "moral excellence." Well! If you're anything like me, you love to strive for excellence. It's inspiring to have a goal, whether it's an "A" on a math quiz or doing your very best in a soccer game, "excellence" is...well, *excellent!* So, in this chapter, I will write about moral excellence, or virtue, and focus especially on those road signs that will guide you toward virtue in your interactions with boys.

Because you know that I love God's Word and His *words,* I get so excited when I learn things about the words that help us to have a more detailed picture of who God is and who He wants us to be. Here's an awesome example from this second chapter of Ruth. The word *virtue* in Hebrew is "chayil," and it also means "strength," "power" and "might." So, being a Young Lady of Virtue is a declaration of your inner strength that is like having "mass army" inside your heart. Our leading man in the Book of Ruth was drawn to the leading lady because of the obvious virtue shown in her life through her actions. It took the strength

Being a Young Lady of Virtue is a declaration of your inner strength that is like having "mass army" inside your heart.

of moral excellence to do the honorable things Ruth did. Now, something very interesting to notice is that one of the Hebrew words used to describe *Boaz* is "chayil"! What it means in the sentence it is used in is that Boaz was a man of power and wealth and a man of virtue. Look at that: A man of virtue was attracted to a young woman of virtue.

Virtue attracted Virtue—we attract our heart's companion.

Why do I want to point this out to you? Because I want you to see that the words and the story are showing us a great truth. Who we are in our hearts—our character—is directly connected to whom we attract. Whether it's our best friends or the man who will someday be your husband, if *you* are a Young Lady of Virtue, you will attract other people of virtue. You will prefer your closest, strongest, most encouraging friendships to be with other people of virtue, of moral excellence. This won't mean that you will not be able to care about and hopefully minister to people who are struggling, even people who are not walking with God; but I'm talking about the people you will make your most important relationships with. Virtue attracts Virtue.

You Are More than Eye Candy

I'll be honest with you—and I am pretty sure I'm not telling you something you don't already know—in the times we live in, virtue is not what most guys are concerned about; they are often too busy looking at the outside of girls and are not even interested in the inside. And *certainly* a Bozo is more focused on how "hot" a girl is than the moral excellence of her heart. So, let's take a closer look at how you can seek to have virtue in some very practical areas of your life.

Help with Modesty

Do you have a "consecrated" closet? To be "consecrated" in biblical words means to be set aside for special use to God. Do you dress modestly, or are you giving more thought to being "eye candy" for the boys around you? These are such hard questions to ask, but girls, I live in South Florida, and what I see at the mall and even at church—much of it looks like it belongs on a beach.

Recently my pastor gave the best explanation of what it is to dress modestly. Dr. Scroggins said, "Modesty is presenting yourself so that the attention of other people is drawn to your *face*." Here's the simple question to ask: What does my outfit draw attention to? Does my outfit show my intent to be modest or does it show that modesty doesn't even exist? And let me assure you of something: You can look totally "adorbs" and wear really cute outfits within the limits of modesty! I *love* clothes! My girlfriends and my daughter and daughter-in-law—we all have as much fun with each other talking about and choosing outfits as any gals do! But I will tell you outright, girls, if you're looking to the fashion of most pop singers or even lots of girls on the Disney Chanel, it's likely you are not seeing examples of modesty. If your shorts or your tops are so short that your underwear is hardly "under" anything...the boys around you are going to have a harder time looking at your face or listening to your words!

Interestingly, speaking of what we wear *under* our clothes, there's a famous store you may know that sells mostly those "under-wears." It's called Victoria's Secret (although I knew a man once who used to turn his head away from those store windows at the mall and say, "Victoria is not keeping her 'secret' very well!"). Just a few years ago, the media paid some attention to a Victoria's Secret model who, as a result of reading the Bible, made a decision to actually *stop* modeling for them. By being a Lady of Faith and studying God's Word, she discovered that it was a conflict to be a follower of Jesus and modeling lingerie (a fancy word for fancy underwear):

> Kylie Bisutti, winner of the 2009 Victoria's Secret Model Search, on why she gave up lingerie modeling. Bisutti continues to model clothing. "My body should only be for my husband. I'm a Christian," she told Fox News, "and reading the Bible more, I was becoming convicted of it."[1]

It is likely that few of us would lose the kind of money and attention that this young lady has committed to because of this choice. In her business, this choice is probably a career killer! Like Ruth, who took the "high road" by following Naomi to Israel, Kylie Bisutti took the high road of virtue by risking her career for the right, moral choice.

Modesty and Tweens and Teens

You might be years away from prom night, but dressing modestly is as *important* an issue in elementary schools as in junior high schools. Virtue and modesty are not just teen issues! God's girls should have wardrobes that prove she is owned by a most holy God, not being controlled by Hollywood! Here is how the Bible says it:

> *Do you not know that your body is a temple of the Holy Spirit who is in you, whom you have from God, and that you are not your own? For you have been bought with a price: therefore glorify God in your body* (1 Corinthians 6:19-20).

We belong to the God who created us and whose Holy Spirit lives within us as Christians. And what is the "price" He bought us with? The blood of Jesus. Jesus gave His life on the cross to pay for our sins. It is for that reason that Paul can write such strong words!

And remember this: Modesty is not attractive to a Bozo. In fact, the good news is that it's another kind of heart guard *against* the Bozo Clan. So your first reason to want to dress modestly is to honor God, who gave His life to clean out the sin in our lives. Your second reason is that our loving heavenly Father wants to *protect* you from the Bozo boys who *do not want* to protect your body, heart, and spirit!

Recently a leader in a Christian school had to discipline several elementary girls for taking inappropriate pictures and texting them to boys at school. The next week this same lady had to discipline an elementary girl for passing a note in Bible class in which she mentioned wanting to do something inappropriate with a particular boy! This Christian-school leader said that in all her years of leadership she had never seen such bold, defiant behavior from little girls (these girls were in fourth and fifth grade). I wanted to scream and cry at the same time when I heard the story! Once again, it's this kind of story that drives me to teach women of all ages to be Women of Virtue—girls and moms—so that we can encourage and help and inspire each other to go a different way than the world.

Who Do Young Ladies of Virtue Date?

You are probably not dating yet—but I want you to know this information *before* you date. On your journey to marriage and family, the kinds of steps you take at ten years old can set the path for your steps at 16 and at 24! One of the earliest things I learned as a new Christian was that I shouldn't date non-Christians. I was at a huge youth leadership retreat when I first heard a teaching on not dating nonbelievers. When the teacher read Second Corinthians 6:14, I knew immediately that I needed to break up with my boyfriend when I returned home. The Word of God hit me *that hard* with truth! I was not from a Christian home, so no one in my family understood why I broke up with him. When I tried to explain, they all shook their heads, disapproving of my decision. It was neither the first nor the last time I would have *that* experience in my family or among my old friends! But through making the best moral choices, God was making me stronger in Him and growing that pearl in my heart.

> *Do not be yoked together with unbelievers. For what do righteousness and wickedness have in common? Or what fellowship can light have with darkness?* (2 Corinthians 6:14 NIV)

I have also had to learn the hard lesson that not every Christian is convinced by God's Word to follow this wisdom. Too often a young girl will say to me, "Well, Mrs. Kendall, I've only had one date with him." I immediately reply, *"Every date is a potential mate. Nobody marries somebody they didn't date!"* It may be tempting to spend time with a guy who doesn't love Jesus. He may be funny or cute or even really nice; but why find yourself getting caught up and attracted to someone who might pull you away from the ultimate reason you're on this planet—to bring Jesus glory?

Toothpicks in Your Eyeballs

Eeeks! What a gross heading! What could I possibly be talking about? Well, the topic of "toothpicks in your eyeballs" is about the pain people give themselves when they disobey the ideas God gives us in the following verses of Scripture:

> *But if you turn away and ally yourselves with the survivors of these nations that remain among you and if you intermarry with them and associate with them, then you may be sure that the Lord your God will no longer drive out these nations before you. Instead, they will become snares and traps for you, whips on your backs and thorns in your eyes...* (Joshua 23:12-13 NIV).

As I mentioned above, when I was a new Christian, I was taught this ancient principle, this very old and important ideal, by one of my spiritual mentors. The principle was simple: Do not date non-believers. I have given this same counsel to many teenage girls and single women throughout the last four decades. Years ago, I wrote about a bride coming down the aisle dressed in a beautiful, white, satin wedding gown—*but,* it was covered in chains and wrapped in a whip. This word picture was based on this same passage of Scripture, because, as you can see, that is what the Lord tells the Israelites will happen if they marry into the other people groups around them—snares and traps, whips and thorns! It is *not* a pretty picture.

Even though this wisdom is clearly stated in both the Old and New Testaments, I still meet women (young and not so young) who think it is only a rule created by the religion of man, and not a *principle* given by our loving, heavenly Father. Sadly, I know many unhappy women who are married to nonbelievers. Time and time again, they admit that they paid no attention to this biblical principle when they were dating. By going against the ideals God teaches in His Word, it's like these women hurt themselves with whips, snares, and thorns in their eyes. When a person goes against the Bible's teachings on purpose, the result is so often self-injury. Remember *God's principles are for our protection*, but it takes faith to believe that God is not trying to take the fun out of life—He is not just out to ruin our day! On the contrary! God's most important ideas, or principles, are designed by *Him* to protect us and bless us.

I always ask women who are married to nonbelievers if anyone warned them about their choices to date and then marry these men. Often they say, "No one challenged me or even warned me about dating a man who didn't know Jesus personally." Don't be a BFF who is too afraid to warn a friend about *not dating* a nonbeliever!

My prayer for you is that you would have the courage of a Micaiah (see 2 Chronicles 18). Do you know who Micaiah is? Micaiah would tell the truth even if the person ended up hating him for what he said. We need courage to speak the truth to any friend who is planning to date a nonbeliever.

We should warn her about the pain of "toothpicks in her eyes." I would rather make a friend miserable for a little while by being honest than to have her spend years in a miserable marriage because I didn't have a "Micaiah spirit" when it came to telling the truth.

We cannot keep teens or young ladies from disobeying God, but we can at least warn them about dangerous, self-harming behaviors on their part. We need to warn them as the apostle Paul did: *"Do not be yoked together with unbelievers"* (2 Corinthians 6:14 NIV). And remember, dating is not just a fun activity. Who you want to date shows where your heart is spiritually. Even if you are years away from dating, the kinds of boys you and your friends spend time with and even "crush on" show what's in your heart. Is the guy you are crushing on in love with Jesus? Remember: Every date is a potential mate, and your mate is one of God's most powerful tools in life for growing you to be more like Him.

Lies Girls Tell Themselves

Do you know what it is to be "deceived"? It's to be led into a lie by someone, to come to believe something that is false. Sometimes, the person who deceives us most is...

Remember: Every date is a potential mate, and your mate is one of God's most powerful tools in life for growing you to be more like Him.

ourselves! And here is an idea that *way* too many girls and women are deceived by: "I have the power to *change* the boy I like." It may be someone she has a crush on, admires from afar, or has begun to date, but it's a lie that many females fall for. I have spoken with thousands of girls who have tried to explain to me why they have a good reason to date non-believers. I have even had girls explain what "nice" guys they are dating. I always ask, "Is he a Christian?"

"Well..." she might answer, "he's a great guy and he comes from a good family."

When I follow up with the second question: "What do you mean by a good family?" I find that, more often than not, *good* means *rich*. Since the first woman, Eve, ate from the forbidden tree, women have thought that they are smarter than God and have the power to change those who become the "objects" of their desire.

Girls, part of why I write is to encourage you to *resist* the fantasy that you can outsmart God.

> *There is no wisdom, no insight, no plan that can succeed against the Lord* (Proverbs 21:30 NIV).

The following true story gives us an example of how girls tend to think and how they really believe they can change another person—especially their future husbands! Pay close attention to who the wisest ones are in the story...

What Even Ninth-Grade Boys Know

My sister-in-law, DeDe, shared a very interesting experience with me about teaching ninth-graders some of the ideas from the book *Lady in Waiting.* The class had both boys and girls in it. She passed out the following list and asked the students to follow the directions at the top:

Put a check beside each of the following characteristics you can change in your husband after marriage:

1. Not willing to talk about important things
2. Bad temper
3. Likes to argue
4. Finds it hard to say "I'm sorry"
5. Bad language
6. Not willing to help with church ministries
7. Not able to keep a job
8. Jealous
9. Self-centered
10. Depressed
11. Not willing to give
12. Wandering eyes (looks at other women)
13. Lying
14. Immature
15. Works too much, does not pay enough attention to his family

DeDe watched, just amazed, as the girls busily checked several of the items on the list above. Ninth-grade girls were already showing how self-deceived they were in thinking one person can change another. After seeing all the checked items on the girls' lists, she noticed that the boys had not checked *any* items on their lists. When asked why they didn't check anything, several boys spoke up saying, "I can't change another person's behavior."

What would you have checked? Would you have answered like those 15-year-old girls, or do you already know what those boys knew? Those were ninth-grade boys who knew they couldn't change a girl, much less a wife someday. The girls in the class were surprised at the boys' comments and began to argue whether people could change "the object of their love." DeDe started laughing as she listened to the girls defend their power to change someone, and the boys' response: "No way!"

Next time someone jokes about how "clueless" boys can be about people, remember this story. These boys showed their wisdom about an important reality in life. Remember this too, though: Even though we can't *make* someone change, we can inspire one another and encourage one another to be excellent in all areas of life. This truth should remind you to be a Young Lady of Diligence, praying to the Lord about wisdom in your friendships and family relationships. Because, let me be crystal clear, dear girls: *Only God can change a person's heart.*

Pray for a "Tigger" in Your Life

When our daughter, Jessi, began seventh grade, she joined the track team. She had run in elementary school, but now she was in junior high, and the training was harder. There was an older girl whom our daughter would tell us about all the time. This wonderful girl always encouraged Jessi when she ran. The girl's cute nickname was "Tigger." Her name was Alicia Tager, so you can see where the nickname came from. We met this encouraging girl at the track meets, and she was a delight to speak to from the moment we met her.

One day our daughter mentioned that Tigger wanted to pick her up early and drive her to school where they could have a short Bible study together. This precious high school girl began picking up our daughter each week. They would then go to the school gym where they would share what they had been reading that week in their Bibles.

As a parent, I had already spent years encouraging Jessi to read her Bible and journal some of her findings—just like I have told you about in Chapter 3. Then, Tigger's encouragement helped Jessi go to an even deeper level in following Jesus. Even after Tigger graduated from high school, she continued to encourage our daughter spiritually.

Do you have a Tigger in your life? If not, start asking Jesus for such an influence. Becoming a Young Lady of Virtue requires all the godly help He sends us. I personally have had several "Tiggers" in my life. We all need someone older and wiser to encourage us to be the dream girl God created us to be (Psalm 139:14).

Are Your Friends Tarnishing Your Virtue?

Did you know that you become like the girls you spend the most time with? Did you know that your BFF is a reflection of who you are becoming? Parents *teach* virtue, but friends either "shine up" or "tarnish" one's virtue. Did you know that your girlfriends help shape your heart? As you befriend, you *become.* Your closest friends give a clue about who you will be in your future.

> *Do not be misled: "Bad company corrupts good character"* (1 Corinthians 15:33 NIV).

Do your friends guide you closer to Jesus or invite you to pull away? Are too many of your friends "lukewarm" spiritually, not caring very much about growing in Jesus? Do you have friends in your life who are like *Daniel's* friends?

I so hope you know who Daniel was in the Bible! Like Ruth, there is an entire book of the Bible named after Daniel that tells important stories about him and his faith—as well as God's faithfulness to him and the Israelites. If you haven't read the story of Daniel, please do! Even a story Bible will give you a great introduction to this mighty young man of faith.

I remember thinking about Daniel, who was called *"a man greatly beloved"* of God (Daniel 10:11 KJV). In the Hebrew, the word translated "beloved" means not only "great delight" and "great desire," but also "delectable." Do you know that word? It really is another word for "delicious."

Wow, Daniel's life was actually "delicious" to God. Think about something you would describe as delicious! Cookies and cream ice cream? Turkey and stuffing covered with gravy? Maybe a favorite kind of pizza! When something is delicious, you look forward to it, you prefer it over other things, you greatly enjoy it, and you can't wait to have more! So, for Daniel to be *delectable* to God meant that God favored him and enjoyed him greatly. Tears filled my eyes as I thought about Daniel, because my heart yearns for my own life to be delectable to God.

As I looked more closely at Daniel's life, I read about his three friends, and the Lord showed me something truly exciting. We know Daniel's friends as Shadrach, Meshach, and Abednego (don't worry if you're not sure how to say those names! They're different than any names we would hear now, that's for sure!), the names they were given when they were all living in captivity in Babylon. However, their not-so-famous Hebrew names were Hananiah, Mishael, and Azariah (more unusual names!). As I studied the Hebrew meanings of these names, I discovered just what kind of friends Daniel had. They are the kind we *all* need—friends who want to follow Jesus with their whole hearts and lives!

- Hananiah means: *The Lord is gracious.*
- Mishael means: *Who is like our God?*
- Azariah means: *The Lord is my help.*

Just imagine! Their names were like messages those friends needed to give one another when all three were pushed into the fiery furnace (see Daniel 3). Their names described the gracious God who cannot be compared to any other—the God who helps His children and who showed up in the furnace as the fourth man. The Lord, who walked through the fire with them, was made up of all three of their names!

Do you have friends who remind you that the Lord is gracious, that He is our helper, and that He is an incomparable God, not able to be compared to any other? Like Daniel's friends were to him, we become a reflection of those people we spend time with (see Amos 3:3; Proverbs 13:20). Does your life reflect that you have the gift of friends like Daniel had? Hananiah, Mishael, and Azariah had their names changed by the men who took them captive to Babylon, but their captors couldn't change their hearts. Their hearts stayed fully committed to their incomparable God!

I would encourage you to start asking God daily for friends like Daniel had and even a special friend like "Tigger" to come into your life and cheer on your virtue and love for Jesus. As you pray to have godly friends and to *be* a godly friend, keep praying to understand what *virtue* means and how to honor God in "moral excellence" in all areas of your life.

Note

1. "Dispatches/Quotables," *World Magazine*, February 25, 2012, 16.

Discussion Questions

Here are some questions you can think about or write about or talk about with someone else. It's not a test! So, feel free to look back in the chapter to help you think about your answers.

1. After reading this chapter, write out what you think the word *virtue* means:
2. Read Ruth 2:10-11. How was Ruth's *virtue* attractive to Boaz?
3. What does it mean that *virtue attracts virtue*?
4. How does your character determine the kind of guy or friend you attract to yourself?
5. How do your clothes show *who you are* and who you *want to attract*? [this is why modesty is important] I Tim. 2:9,10
6. Why is it so important for you to someday date a guy who is a passionate follower of Christ? (instead of a guy who calls himself a "Christian" but lives like everyone else)
7. Think about your closest, best friends. How do they push you *towards* or *away* from God?

Chapter 5

Becoming a Young Lady of Devotion

Rescue me from me that I might serve Thee. –JMK

Ruth's Devotion

One of the reasons I love words is that they can be like a treasure hunt. When I don't really understand what a word means I can look it up and see what other words it comes from. Let's look at this word *devotion*, because you probably have an idea what it means, but to see the words it comes from gives us a great word picture! To begin with, it comes from the word *devote*. If you break apart that word, you get "de" and "vote." The first syllable, *de*, means "down" in this word (like to *de*scend a staircase), and the next syllable is a word we all know, *vote*. Vote comes from the same word as "vow," like to take a vow or make a promise. Well, now we have "down-vow," which sounds sort of odd, but you can actually begin to see the word picture, because when this word was made up in Latin, more than a thousand years ago, that meant to *bow down and make a vow.* So now you can see that to "devote" yourself to someone is to make a solemn or serious promise to give your best attention to that person. You can understand why this word is most often used about our relationship to God. To be *devoted* to God is to bow before Him in our hearts and to promise our most focused attention and most heartfelt worship and most dedicated service.

We know that Ruth was a woman of devotion to the God of Israel—her words *and* her actions spoke loudly of that! As I have written in earlier chapters, it was her devotion that attracted Boaz to Ruth, because her devotion to God is what inspired her to be diligent and to have virtue. Boaz spoke of Ruth's devotion to God when he said:

> *May the Lord reward your work, and your wages be full from the Lord, the God of Israel, under whose wings you have come to seek refuge* (Ruth 2:12).

I had been reading and studying the Book of Ruth for more than 40 years before I really noticed the word *reward* in the verse above. I started to look more closely at what Boaz was saying to Ruth in their very first meeting. Boaz was

*To be **devoted** to God is to bow before Him in our hearts and to promise our most focused attention and most heartfelt worship and most dedicated service.*

speaking a blessing over Ruth. He was speaking a prayer over her about God "rewarding" Ruth for choosing to hide under God's wings. Boaz was praying that God would *reward* Ruth's *hope* in the God of Israel, in other words, to reward her devotion to Him.

The word *reward* in Hebrew is also translated "to pay back" or "repay." Boaz is praying that God would *pay Ruth back* for fleeing to Him for protection and hope. Isn't that the coolest thought? God rewards us when we come to Him for hope at those times when our lives feel hopeless. I have often felt spoiled by God, by the wonderful family and friends He has given me and the many amazing ministry experiences He has led me to; but this verse reminded me of the many times I have run to God in tears, and He heard my cry and rewarded my fleeing to Him. You remember the story I wrote about my "date with Jesus" when the rainbow and the full moon came out? That was a time I ran to the Lord and He "paid me back" with blessings.

I could fill a book with stories that fit this topic! Once, I was so mad at a certain woman who had said some pretty mean things about me and people I loved. The report of her unkindness (and untruth) shook me up so much, I just wanted to get revenge! In the middle of my fit, when I was determined to go find her and give her a "piece of my mind," I could not find my car keys. Well, running around looking for the keys gave the Holy Spirit just enough time to speak to my heart, "Pray for her, Jackie!"—and by His power, I did. I stopped running out of my house and ran, instead, to God!

In faith, I prayed for her and I told the Lord how hurt and angry I was…and do you know what the Spirit of God led me to do? I was reminded of a Bible verse I had memorized years before that told me to *bless* and not *curse* my "enemies," and that it was God's business to "get even" with someone—to pay them back for their bad choices. And so, led by Jesus, I went to the store and bought this lady a gift. In fact, I bought her something that I had wanted to buy for myself earlier that week! I even had it gift-wrapped. Then, I had it sent to her. I went to the Lord for "refuge," for safety, when I was so upset, and He rewarded me with clear marching orders that reflected His heart, not my upset.

That's not the end of the story, though! A young woman called me to see what I had done to "get back" at the woman I was so mad at. What a faithful sister to check in with me and make sure I had not done anything foolish! I told her what the Lord had led me to do and how He brought peace and joy back to my heart by acting in obedience to Him. *She* then told the story to her mother, her mother who was so full of doubts about God. And do you know what? That mom was just shocked that anyone would buy a gift for someone who had said mean things about them. She saw that only God could cause someone to do such a thing, and she said it was the most powerful witness to the love of Jesus she had seen. *This* was a great reward to me, as I had been praying for this woman, too. Isn't it awesome that we never know *how* Jesus will use our obedience to His Word and *who* might be touched by it…but we can know that He will reward us for our hope in Him and keep our eyes open for what that reward might be!

Do You Run to God When You're Upset?

Now, who runs to God when they are upset? Many people run to God when they are having trouble, like a bad health problem or serious worries about money, but the Young Lady of Devotion has confidence in the One she is running to with her tears—no matter if they are tears of sadness or loneliness or anger. *And*, such devotion gives you the courage and strength to keep trusting God with your tears even when the problem is not solved right away.

One time my daughter, Jessi, got some terribly sad news on the phone. She burst right into tears and slid down the cabinet onto the kitchen floor weeping hysterically! As she was weeping, she suddenly heard the pounding of her little three-year-old daughter's feet running to the kitchen. When Jessi looked up through her blinding tears, she saw her precious Emma holding her own little Bible, ready to hand it to her mommy. Jessi had not asked Emma to go get her Bible; Emma heard her mama crying and at such a young age *already understood* that the Father of *all comfort* (see 2 Corinthians 1:3) uses the Bible to comfort His kids. "Oh, yes, baby girl!" Jessi said to her daughter, "God's Word is the only thing that will put me back on my feet."

> *My soul weeps because of grief; strengthen me according to Your word* (Psalm 119:28).

When you have a friend crying, do you run for the Word like little Emma? The Young Lady of Devotion knows where to run when trouble comes, because she knows the following promise in God's Word:

> *Let us then approach God's throne of grace with confidence, so that we may receive mercy and find grace to help us in our time of need* (Hebrews 4:16 NIV).

Can you think of the last time you were crying? Did you talk to Jesus about the tears and your need for help? Did you talk to your mom or your BFF but didn't even think about talking to Jesus about your problem? My hope for you is that you will learn to run and hide "under the wings," as the Scripture says, of our mighty God. And here is something you may not even know—that the Lord wants us to come to Him with our troubles! It is no small part of being devoted to Him to bring our cares and our tears to His throne in prayer, because by doing this, we are bowing down and saying, "Papa God, *You* are God! I need Your help and Your comfort and Your wisdom." You see? When we do this we are putting ourselves, as His creation, in our right place with God, our Creator—completely dependent on Him. *This* is the safe place He wants us to be!

God is your safest place to run and to hide. He loves you *so dearly.* However, it's a sad…no, a *tragic* fact that many people have very negative ideas about our loving God in their heads. Ruth had to choose to follow God even though Naomi had drawn a negative, harsh picture of Him. Here is what she said to her two daughters-in-law:

> *Do not call me Naomi; call me Mara, for the Almighty has dealt very bitterly with me. I went out full, but the Lord has brought me back empty. Why do you call me Naomi, since the Lord has witnessed against me and the Almighty has afflicted me?* (Ruth 1:20-21)

Who would choose to be devoted to a God like Naomi describes here? Naomi, who was in grief and, as we can understand, upset, was not turning *to God* for comfort, but turning *away from* God by stating that He was a cruel God. Because Ruth had learned about the Lord in her years of being married into a Jewish family, she was now making a choice *not* to accept Naomi's bitter view of God for herself. Ruth's devotion to God allowed her to look past her mother-in-law's bitter remarks about God.

*That is what **devotion** gives your heart—confidence, even in a crowd of cranky, faithless people.*

Your growing devotion to God can help you to look past negative remarks about God—whether they come from family or friends, or from movies or music. If Ruth kept her focus on God even when Naomi was really upset and not describing the true heart of God, you, too, can learn to focus on the goodness of God, even when people in your family or some of your friends don't share your confidence about God. That is what *devotion* gives your heart—confidence, even in a crowd of cranky, faithless people.

Your Devotion Affects Those around You

While devotion to God is an *every*day virtue, how we respond to Him in tough times shows our faith. Are you an example of hope in God when you are having difficult times at home or at school? Do the kids around you know that even when times are hard, you, like Ruth, flee to God for help? Would others describe you more like Ruth, devoted to God even in difficult circumstances, or more like Naomi, who was angry at God? When Naomi said, in the verse quoted above, that she wanted to be called "Mara," which means "bitter," it was because she had become bitter during her difficult trials. I am not saying that Naomi didn't have a terrible situation that I could hardly imagine having to face! But her choice was to "awefulize" her life, completely shutting down to her God. Do you know people who "awefulize" everything that goes wrong? Things "stink" or are "the worst" for people who awefulize. Life seems like one crisis after another for someone with this mindset—and if we get sucked into it, we can become bitter like Naomi. That bitter attitude can affect the people around us as much, if not more, than our hope in God.

Devotion and Kisses on One's Hand and Arm

Do you have a bedtime ritual that you do almost every night before you go to sleep? My little granddaughter loves to remind me that, before she can go to sleep, she must:

1) read a Bible story, 2) pray, and 3) sing a worship song. After I finished reading the Bible story one night, I had Emma lie down, and I knelt by her tiny bed and began to pray. As soon as I finished praying, I heard Emma's sweet voice say, "Don't forget to sing, Mimi." I asked Emma what song she would like me to sing, and she replied, "How Great Is Our God." Now, I have to admit, I have a pitiful singing voice, but as I began to sing, tears began to roll down my cheeks just thinking about the honor of singing over my grandbaby. As I closed my eyes to sing, I raised one hand to the Lord in worship. Suddenly I felt Emma grab my other hand and begin to kiss it! Then she kissed my arm! When I finished singing, Emma said, "I love you Mimi." As I kissed her goodnight, the Lord put this thought into my heart: God wants me to walk with such bold devotion to Him that people will see my devotion and want to "kiss God's hand."

> *Let us go with you, for we have heard that God is with you* (Zechariah 8:23).

Mission Fields at the Front Door of Your Life

As a growing Young Lady of Devotion, Jesus wants you to be very aware that the different kids who come into your life are there for a very important kind of friendship. Some of the kids you will attract have been brought into your life to encourage them to either come to know Jesus or grow deeper in their devotion to Jesus. In fact, if you have a Christian family, your circle of friends is like a "mission field" for you and your family. A college girl named Crystal shared an important truth when she was telling us how she came to know Jesus. I wanted to post it on the hearts of all the moms and daughters I know. Crystal said:

> "I came to *know* the Lord at a youth camp, but I came to *love* the Lord through the Jacob family."

Crystal spent time with a Christian family, the Jacobs, who showed her what it was like to be loved by Jesus *and* how to love others like Jesus. Like that family, you and your family will be blessed by encouraging other kids in their devotion to God. You may want to read and discuss the following paragraphs with your mom or dad. *Why?* So that you and your parents can be a "tag-team" in caring for the kids God is bringing into your life at school and at church. These words are from my book *Raising a Lady in Waiting*:

> Your children will attract a variety of young people who might end up in your living room. When the mission field comes through your door, you may be tempted to say, "Oh no, I don't like that boy or girl."
>
> Reflect before you respond. *Pray* before you react. Be careful not to reject the child quickly, because he or she has been delivered to your family room by the Holy One. Your first response may be, "Not this type of child, Lord! Isn't it time for her to go home?"

> You cannot love your kids' friends to Jesus without accepting them where they are and praying for where they need to go. When you and I learn to do both, we will effectively fulfill our place in this mission field that God delivered to us.

Needy kids are always drawn to kids who have what I call "God-confidence." Young people struggle a lot with insecurity, and a growing Young Lady of Devotion will always present confidence in her daily walk and attract some more insecure kids. Ask God how to care for those kids and how to show each one the love of Jesus.

If we don't love others, they'll never believe that God loves them.

Prayer Requests in a Photo Album

Take a minute and think about all the kids and adults you know at church and at school. Each of these people needs prayer, and you have the honor as a growing Young Lady of Devotion to learn how to pray regularly for the people you know—whether young or old. This activity will not only strengthen your diligence (remember Chapter 2?) but also be a blessing to God in your devotion to Him.

Ask God how to care for those kids and how to show each one the love of Jesus.

Because I have a brain that is easily distracted (I wonder if anyone can relate?), I came up with a creative way to help me remember to pray for many of the kids and adults needing prayer in my life. I bought two things—a package of 4×6 index cards and a 4×6 plastic photo album (I got a really cheap one from the dollar store). I wrote out some categories for my prayer requests, which I will list below. Then, I put the prayer cards in the photo album to keep them in good shape. Each card became a holy reminder to pray, and it has helped me *so* much to stay consistent in praying.

Here is a list of categories. You could write each heading on a card and then put people's names and prayer needs under the right category. I might have a few cards with the same heading if there are a number of people who fit that category.

1. Family members
2. BFF
3. Kids who need Jesus
4. Friends whose parents are going through a divorce
5. Spiritual leaders at your church and school
6. Missionaries you might know
7. Mean girls who need a healed heart
8. Former BFF

First of all, then, I urge that entreaties and prayers, petitions and thanksgivings, be made on behalf of all men (1 Timothy 2:1).

You will probably think of another category, but these will at least help you get started!

Finding My Prince and My Devotion to God

As you follow the road signs on your journey toward marriage, the very best choice you can make to attract a prince who also has a connection with God's heart is to be a Young Lady of Devotion. Your devotion to God will cause you to be attracted to a Boaz who cheers you on *toward* God instead of a Bozo who pulls you away from Him. In fact, this bit of truth is not only about dating but also friendship. I am always asking the same questions to the teens I meet across this nation: "Does your boyfriend help you to grow closer to God? Or do you find yourself stepping backward and losing interest in the Bible, in prayer, in youth group? Are you hanging around your Christian friends less and less because of this boy's influence?"

I also ask younger girls questions like: "Does your best friend love Jesus? Is she a growing Christian? Does your BFF know the difference between a Bozo and a Boaz? Do you and your BFF talk about the Lord and what He is doing in your life?"

Does your BFF know the difference between a Bozo and a Boaz?

Here is how an Old Testament prophet, Malachi, describes what God does with our discussions about Him. He keeps a "scroll of remembrance," which is what I think of as a heavenly journal.

> *Then those who feared the Lord talked with each other, and the Lord listened and heard. A scroll of remembrance was written in his presence concerning those who feared the Lord and honored his name* (Malachi 3:16 NIV).

Isn't that amazing? Not only does God hear us, but He writes in His journal when we *bless Him* by encouraging each other and sharing about Him with one another. Friends can be the best kind of cheerleaders for each others' spiritual growth; and by blessing each other, they bring God so much joy that He writes about it in His "scroll of remembrance." The opposite of this is also true, I'm sorry to say. Kids can also tease and tear down each others' devotion. So, if you practice helping your friends now, at your age, be stronger and stronger followers of Jesus, you are learning the best kind of habit for when you are a teenager. As you grow closer to God, you and your girlfriends are growing into the kinds of girls who will attract a prince, like Boaz.

Deliver Us from the "Kingdom of Self"

Now, to grow in devotion to the Lord is to focus on Him and to seek His heart for His Kingdom. Yet, as we all know, there is another kingdom we like to visit—in fact, we like to camp out there, sometimes for long periods of time! It is not the beautiful, enormous Kingdom of God, but the ugly, tiny "Kingdom of Self." I think of this "kingdom" like a small, dark closet in the back corner of a nasty, damp basement. Sadly, we can get very comfortable in this dark hole and don't even realize how cramped it is.

When I became a new Christian, I was told that I could either live a life with *Self* in charge or the Holy Spirit in charge. I was constantly asked by my youth leader whether the things I did were led by *Self* being on the throne of my life or by the guidance of the Holy Spirit. The Bible clearly says what this Kingdom of Self looks like:

> *Now the works of the flesh are obvious: sexual immorality, impurity, depravity, idolatry, sorcery, hostilities, strife, jealousy, outbursts of anger, selfish rivalries, dissensions, factions, envying, murder, drunkenness, carousing, and similar things* (Galatians 5:19-21 NET).

You may not know all of these terms, and some may seem very far from your life experience, yet it's important to go back to this Scripture at different times in life to see the behaviors of the me-centered life that is at war with the life of God within each of His children. If you read the words you do know—like jealousy, anger, selfishness, envy—you will understand that everything this Scripture warns us about has to do with selfish sin. These are ways of thinking and acting that put *Me* at the center of my choices. If I get furious at my little sister (what is called "outbursts of anger"),

I am spilling anger all over the place without thinking how it might feel to her to be yelled at. If someone creates problems between two or three friends by telling them some mean thing another friend said, that's called "strife," and we tend to make strife between people because it makes us look cool somehow. Even getting drunk is a *me*-centered activity. People say terrible things and do stupid things when they're drunk. Worse, they can drive and smash into another car! Getting drunk makes people even more me-centered than they already were. This is why the Bible warns against it a number of times.

From time to time on long trips in the car, I listen to a radio program with a doctor who gives advice for people's problems. It always makes me grin when the doctor says to an upset caller, "Now just a minute, I need you to take yourself out of the center of your universe and take a moment to think about this other person." *Ha!* We all need to be reminded to get *off* the throne of our own lives and to come *out* of the dark Kingdom of Self.

Rescue Me from Me

Being delivered from me-centered life in the Kingdom of Self takes practice and it means that someone needs to *choose* to leave! Me-centered girls are so self-focused that they don't like limits. Resisting limits affects the way they respond to parents and teachers, and also shows up in their behavior toward boys.

When a girl is imprisoned in the Kingdom of Self, she is not willing to be careful around someone who's not good for her. She doesn't want to be told that this cute, funny, popular guy is a Bozo, because *she wants what she wants when she wants it!* Sometimes the boy isn't even good-looking or charming, but he just pays a lot of attention to her. Her me-centered heartbeat cheers her on to get what she wants no matter what. "I want it. I deserve to be happy. This boy's attention will make me happy!"

I hear it said *all the time*: "I just want to be happy." *Happy* becomes the most important thing in life instead of the biblical teaching of devotion to Jesus! A growing Young Lady of Devotion knows that true lasting happiness comes from her growing devotion to Jesus.

Me-Centered Attitude Cancels God-Centered Gratitude

In the Book of Ruth, after amazing kindness was shown to Ruth by the stranger, Boaz, her instant response was what I like to call "high-five" gratitude. You know when something so exciting happens, like your team getting a goal in a game, and you are *so* psyched you just jump up and high-five the closest person? That's the kind of "This is *awesome!*" amazement Ruth experienced in gratitude to Boaz—so grateful that, as you'll see, she falls right to the ground! *Ha!* Yes! You or I might run over to someone and high-five them and hug them and say over and over, "Thank you! Thank you! Thank you so much!" The ancient version of that was to fall on your face in humble thanks. And that's just what Ruth did.

For the me-centered girl, amazing kindness and goodness don't inspire such gratitude, for this simple reason: The me-centered girl thinks the world spins around her, so there's no need for gratitude. Kids who skip around in the Kingdom of Self may never notice the loving and kind actions of those around them, because they see everyone as their willing servants. When was the last time you felt "high-five gratitude"? Have you thanked your parents recently for all they have done for you? Have you thanked your BFF for being such a good friend? Have you thanked your youth pastor for all his encouragement? To grow in an "attitude of gratitude" comes from giving thanks to others—often!

And let me add this important note. You may not come from a family that practices thanking each other much, so you may not be used to saying *thank you* to your parents or brothers and sisters, much less your friends or teachers. It can feel awkward at first, just like any new thing you are trying out. This is a great place to ask God for His help to give you courage and humility! Pray that Jesus would show

When was the last time you felt "high-five gratitude"? Have you thanked your parents recently for all they have done for you?

you who to thank, for what kinds of things, and what words to use. Did you know that you can also ask someone you trust, like a pastor or a family member, to help you learn to be more grateful? I'm totally serious. You would bless someone if you asked for his or her help to know what to thank people for—or even what to thank God for! Before long, showing your gratitude will be a great habit you look forward to practicing!

Listen to the words of Ruth with her beautiful ability to express gratitude:

> *At this, she bowed down with her face to the ground. She asked him, "Why have I found such favor in your eyes that you notice me—a foreigner?"* (Ruth 2:10 NIV)

Ruth's response to Boaz was gratitude that came from her devotion to the one true God. Young people are definitely able to be full of great unselfishness and devotion to Jesus. I shared with you in Chapter 2 about Katie who moved to Africa to take care of orphans. I would expect that if we met Katie, we would find her to be a young woman with a lot of gratefulness in her heart.

I know a young woman named Chelsea who came from very painful past. There were times when I wasn't sure she would heal from the terrible heart wound she had. But Chelsea was challenged to *think of others* instead of just thinking, "poor me." And this precious girl blossomed like a lovely flower into a soft-hearted, devoted follower of Jesus.

One time I asked her how her fund raising was going for her summer mission trip. She needed to raise $5,000, and said she had all her money and was now helping her best friend to raise her money. I was stunned! How on earth had she already raised that much money? "Oh!" she said with excitement, "I was given $5,000 for graduation and that's the money I am using to pay for my trip to Uganda."

Not only was I blown away that Chelsea used her graduation gift to go on a mission trip (instead of spending it all on me-centered *things*), but I was also blessed by her devoted passion to help her friend raise funds for *her* mission trip. Talk about cheering on another person's devotion to God!

Chelsea's sad and difficult life could have totally fed the me-centered idol of Self. She especially could have tried to heal her wounded heart through selfishness. Instead, this beautiful young woman went to a very difficult place on her summer vacation to love children in Uganda who have had similar heart wounds. Chelsea's spiritual mom has cheered on her devotion to God for more than ten years, and the results still bring tears to my eyes!

Glory Robber vs. the Young Lady of Devotion

God has made us to be bright reflections of Him in the world. Whenever you are thoughtful or loving, joyful or full of praise, it is a quality of *God's nature* shining through you. The Bible says that God created us to shine with His "glory." *Glory* is really a fabulous word, because it sums up all that is magnificent and excellent and beautiful about God—and the Lord allows even imperfect sinners to show signs of what is glorious about Him. This gets me so excited I could jump up and down! Actually, I *do* jump up and down sometimes when I am worshiping Jesus, because I am so in awe that He entrusts us with this honor—to bring Him glory!

We had a young guest stay with us one summer who was such a blessing that her visit seemed much too short. During hours of sharing heart to heart, I told her about a new message I was writing called "Glory Robbers." I explained that, although we were created to bring God glory, we constantly rob Him of the glory that should be His. Too many Christians have made their lives so me-centered that they daily rob His glory. We don't give God the credit for all the blessings He gives us and we can be ungrateful...and even forget about God completely in our daily lives. When we give in to our old, sinful ways, we miss opportunities to shine with God's glory by acting like Him with love and patience, kindness and courage.

After our wonderful guest left, she gave more thought to this image of a "Glory Robber," and she wrote to tell me a story that perfectly fit the idea. She had been a bridesmaid in a wedding, and as all the girls were getting ready, she noticed that they were much more worried about how *they* looked than with helping the precious bride get ready or serving her needs. Some bridesmaids were only around when the pictures were being taken or when the video camera was on, but nowhere to be found when the hall needed cleaning or the trucks needed packing. These me-centered young women were looking for the "glory" and hoping that people would notice them...but they were robbing the glory that was due to the bride and groom by serving them on their most special day.[1]

Well, did you know that the Church is called the "Bride of Christ" in the Bible? And, of course, Jesus is the heavenly Groom. So, this wise young woman understood that Christians act just like those bridesmaids, looking to get their own glory when they only serve God if it serves them! If someone only helps out at church if she will get "credit" in a special way or if she disappears during a church-wide work day, but shows up for the pictures that will be in the slide show, this is what it is to be a Glory Robber. What if a girl were asked to help in the nursery one Sunday, but knows that her Sunday School class is getting ice cream that day and says "no" to helping. Is that being a Glory Robber? I would say "yes!" Any time we look first and foremost to what we get out of something and don't look to serve the Lord and shine for Him, we are acting like Glory Robbers!

> *Everyone who is called by my name, whom I created for my glory...* (Isaiah 43:7 NIV).

Let's not be like the me-centered bridesmaids in the story above. May we resist the temptation of just serving to get credit or when it's easy for us, and let's ask God to help us be true servants of the King. Such servants are willing to think of others as more important than themselves (see Philippians 2:3).

The Young Lady of Devotion knows how to bring glory to God and not rob Him of such glory! May you, by God's grace, be girls who are God-glorifying Young Ladies of Devotion.

> *"Because he is **lovingly devoted** to Me, I will deliver him;*
> *I will protect him because he knows My name.*
> *When he calls out to me, I will answer him;*
> *I will be with him in trouble,*
> *I will rescue him and give him honor"*
> (Psalm 91:14-15 HCSB).

Note

1. C.V., personal note to author, July 2010.

Discussion Questions

Here are some questions you can think about or write about or talk about with someone else. It's not a test! So, feel free to look back in the chapter to help you think about your answers.

1. What way was Ruth devoted to God?
2. Why is it so important to run to God when you are upset? How can His Word help you during difficult times? (just like it did for my daughter Jessi) Psalm 63
3. How can your devotion to God be an example to the people around you?
4. Your circle of friends, in some ways, can look like a *mission field.* Think of some of the people that God has brought into your life especially so *you* could show His love and kindness to them.

   Write down their names and pray for them. Ask God for ways you can specifically share His love with them.
5. How can you share God's love with these people *without* making the poor choices that they are?
6. What are some ways to get over being self-centered and self-focused?

Chapter 6

Becoming a Young Lady of Purity

A girl's purity is, in fact, a lifelong guard of her heart. –JMK

Ruth's Purity

> *When Boaz had eaten and drunk and his heart was merry, he went to lie down at the end of the heap of grain; and she came secretly, and uncovered his feet and lay down* (Ruth 3:7).

Well, *this* sounds like a bizarre thing to do! If this scene were in a movie, you might think your dad would fast-forward right about now to skip past something you shouldn't see! But here's what was happening—and there's nothing "R-rated" about it. Ruth was acting in obedience to her mother-in-law's instructions and was following the customs of her time. The reason she lay quietly at his feet was for him to notice her when he awoke. This was an action that showed Boaz she was submitting to him, because he was a relative of Naomi's family who could help Ruth. In the Bible, Boaz is called her "kinsman redeemer," which means that he was "kin" to her (a relative) and he could choose to legally "redeem" Ruth and Naomi, which means to take them in to his home to care for them. Basically, Ruth was saying to this man, "I offer myself to be your servant and ask for your protection and care." She was offering to be his wife, too, if that's what he wanted (though a man could take widows into his home without marrying one of them). You'll see in Chapter 7, when we pick up at this point in Ruth's story, that Boaz was very honored by Ruth's actions.

So, this was not an inappropriate act. It truly was an act of obedience to God's plan for Ruth and Naomi to be provided for in those ancient days. One thing is certain. When she left Boaz that morning to go home, she walked away as a Lady of Purity.

Young Lady of Purity in the 21st Century

Someone might take a look at this section title and cry out, "Are you kidding?! This is totally unrealistic! Purity in *this* day and age? Whatever!" You know why they'd say that. Is it even possible for girls (or boys) to stay sexually pure in a society that shows off sexuality everywhere—on TV, YouTube, movies, magazines at the grocery story, even in the classrooms and on the campuses of your schools? I want you to hear something "loud and clear"! If it really weren't possible for anyone to stay pure until marriage in our culture, then I'm just wasting my time sharing the story of Boaz and Ruth as an ideal. It would just be a fairy tale! An idea that belongs in a Disney cartoon! But girls, I am here to tell you that I know tons of young women and guys who have stayed pure and saved their sexual relationship for marriage. I believe with my whole heart that a Young Lady of Purity can live a very fulfilled life in the 21st century.

Just as Ruth's commitment to purity allowed her to go to Boaz at night, ask that he might be her kinsman redeemer, and then leave as pure as she entered, girls can keep their purity even when that is greatly challenged all around them.

I am pretty sure that a girl reading this book has been taught some things about the very important relationship that God created men and women to share in marriage. But I also know that girls learn lots of different things—some things from their parents, some from church, and some from school. I *so* don't want to embarrass anyone in this chapter… yet, I *so* want you to know that *you have a treasure.* A treasure to guard and to give. This treasure is your deepest heart and your precious body. Can you think of any parts of yourself more special than your heart and your body? To grow through the years of being a teenager (which you almost are!) is to learn how to be friends with boys in ways that *guard* yourself so that you can *give* yourself to the prince God has for you in your future. If the Lord brings you a prince of a

*Learn how to be friends with boys in ways that **guard** yourself so that you can **give** yourself to the prince God has for you in your future.*

husband, then you will give your heart and body to him. No matter what happens in our lives, our heart and our bodies belong to our heavenly Prince, the Prince of Peace—Jesus!

> *Do you not know that your bodies are temples of the Holy Spirit, who is in you, whom you have received from God? You are not your own; you were bought at a price. Therefore honor God with your bodies* (1 Corinthians 6:19-20 NIV).

Necessary Pre-Dating Prep

When you read the Bible verse above, can you picture that your body is a beautiful temple or church that was built by God for His Spirit to live in? It might be a fun and helpful activity to look online for pictures of the most gorgeous churches—like cathedrals—and see the kind of stunning designs the builders made in the carvings and the stained glass. *You*, your body, God says, was made to be such a place, made especially for Him. Can you imagine if someone dumped truckloads of trash in a church or took spray paint and wrote curse words all over the inside of one of those cathedrals? Can you imagine if you went in with jackhammers and sledgehammers and smashed all the windows and the marble?

It might sound like a ridiculous exaggeration! But this is *exactly* what we do when we destroy God's "temple" by going against His purpose for our bodies in sexual relationships. What a Young Lady of Purity needs to know *first and foremost* is that God clearly made sex for marriage. God's will about sex before marriage is spelled out—crystal clear—in First Thessalonians 4:3-5:

> *It is God's will that you should be sanctified: that you should avoid sexual immorality; that each of you should learn to control your own body in a way that is holy and honorable, not in passionate lust like the pagans, who do not know God* (NIV).

This is the will of God, that you *abstain* from sexual immorality. To "abstain" is to *not do* something, to stay away from doing it. So, purity is the will of God. It is God's will, no exceptions. And as Young Ladies of Total Surrender and Young Ladies of Devotion who are learning to follow the will of God, you can yell "Amen!" to our heavenly Father's guidelines—*abstain.*

So, that's pretty clear, wouldn't you say? (Even though people can make it pretty complicated!) And for you, who may not be ready to date boys for four, five, six years...you are learning *now* that purity is a lifelong practice! At your age, the practice of purity includes what we already covered in Chapter 4 about virtue, like how you choose to dress and who you follow as your role models in that area of life. In Chapter 2, "Diligence," do you remember learning about how to *pray* for a boy you might have a little "crush" on? As I wrote there, if you think about a boy a lot and try to get his attention, you make him a "big deal" in your thoughts—and that's *not* a practice of purity. But if you tell Jesus how you feel, and pray for the boy, and practice putting aside the thoughts that might come into your head about him, *that* builds the muscles of a pure mind. A pure mind, totally surrendered to Jesus, is the number-one protector of a pure heart and body!

These are the practices of a Young Lady of Purity. In fact, most everything you are reading in this book connects to having a pure heart, mind, and body, because you are growing in your devotion to the Lord—and that is the *best* preparation for dating...and marriage.

The Law of Diminishing Returns

It really is "a must" that a Young Lady of Purity understand this pre-dating preparation. And now I want to explain to you one of the *most important* ideas for that prep. This is what I call "The Law of Diminishing Returns." What? Is that some math thing? What is Mrs. Kendall talking about now? *Ha!* Well, don't panic, girls, because I am going to explain this "Law" to you in a lot of detail. It is a principle that has everything to do with a girl's purity. In fact, in my opinion, a teenage girl should not be allowed to date until she understands the Law of Diminishing Returns. You may not be a teen yet, but you are going to be an even *smarter* teen because you have learned these ideas early, in preparation.

You know that I like to break things down to explain them, so I'll begin by doing that with the name of this Law.

"Law" is a way to name an idea that's true. Sure, there's the law that we follow in our towns (don't speed, pay your taxes) but a Law with a title is usually a name for something that always happens, something that you can count on. Here's an example: the Law of Gravity. And what does that tell us? Simply that things fall *down* and not up! It's so predictable that it can be called a Law. Here's another one: the Law of the Jungle. Now *that* idea is that the strongest, most ferocious animals—like lions—go after weaker animals—like zebras. So, this thing I'm going to tell you about is a Law that is a predictable and true thing.

What about that word *diminishing*? I bet you know that it means "to get smaller" or "to shrink." So, that's a simple part of the title. And then we have the word *returns*. In this case, a "return" is a term used in banking. If I invest a certain amount of money that earns interest (extra money), the extra money is my "return." Well, if this Law is about returns that *diminish*, what does that tell you? You're right! The extra amount gets smaller! *The Law of Diminishing Returns is the fact that there are certain situations where you invest or give something and you end up getting less and less back*. Let's see how that has *anything* to do with the purity of a girl's mind and body, because I will tell you, it has *everything* to do with it!

Do you remember the first time you went somewhere you were just *so* excited about—maybe an amusement park, perhaps even a big one like Disney World or Six Flags? All your senses were alert to take in the experience in as many ways as you could. The colors were bright and fun, the rides were a thrill, the food was simply delicious! It was fabulous! Now imagine that in the next few years, you have gone again…and again. And while you might still enjoy that roller coaster or still really like the familiar taste of that "favorite" chocolate ice cream cake, it's not what you would call a big thrill anymore.

This is an example of the Law of Diminishing Returns. The return you get from your experience gets less and less intense over time. *It loses some of its "Wow!" factor.*

The Law of Diminishing Returns: Avoiding the No Zone

Because of how God created us, for all young people (Christian or not) there is a natural path of the body's sexual experience. When that path is taken to its end, though, *outside of marriage*, it is sin. If a couple walks down that path together all the way to the edge, they will find they have gone much too far! This sexual sin begins with what seems "cute and innocent" and ends up hurting both of them in deep ways. So what does that path look like? Here is a list that describes some of the steps on that path that people will push through *because* of what you learned above—the Law of Diminishing Returns. They will give up on pure thoughts and actions and keep going to the next step so they can feel the thrill of their first trip to Six Flags all over again.

Path to Sexual Sin:

1. Looking at each other
2. Thoughts about each other
3. Touch, like holding hands lightly
4. Holding hands constantly
5. Hugging
6. Long Hugs
7. Light kiss
8. Strong kissing
9. Entering the *No Zone*—area below the neck

Now I'll tell you a story that will show you *exactly* how the Law of Diminishing Returns might work in real life.

A mom drops off her daughter at the mall. Let's call the girl "Molly." Maybe Molly told her mom that she was going to meet up with her girlfriends. Maybe she didn't tell the truth, because it really is a boy she's crushing on who invited her to the mall. Most parents feel safe when their child is in public at the mall. But as you will see, the Law of Diminishing Returns is predictable even in the crowded mall.

What would tempt Molly to not tell her mom about meeting this boy at the mall? (By the way, the boy needs a name, too, so how about "Tyler"?) If you look at the list above, you can imagine that Tyler's not just a kid Molly says "Hi" to in the cafeteria. Molly and Tyler have been watching each other—closely! They have already moved from watching each other to thinking about each other, and probably a lot! You don't just "get" a crush on a boy the way you "get" a cold. That's like the term "falling" in love. No! These are states of mind and heart that we build by thinking about the other person, over and over again. Girls are experts at thinking a boy right into marriage—when she's only 13 years old and hasn't even spent an hour with him! She already knows what color her bridesmaids' dresses will be. She's already doodling the names of their babies on her geometry notebook. All this has happened in her pretty little head, and all by herself.

So, by the time Tyler asks her to go to the mall, Molly might be willing to lie to her parents and say she's meeting her girlfriends *exactly* because she has such a crush on Tyler and *knows* that her desires for his special attention are not really so pure. Think about this, girls—if he were just her friend's brother or just a pal from youth group, there would've been no reason to cover up the truth that he was going to be with her friends at the mall. But Molly is captivated by Tyler. All her staring at him and thinking about him now has her held captive to the idea of "something" more.

Even if Molly's parents know she is meeting Tyler there, they think these kids are "just going to walk around the mall together." It all seems innocent, right? What kind of trouble could anyone get into? So now, as they are strolling around, Tyler reaches over and takes Molly's hand. As sweet as this act of affection may seem, you have no idea how powerful that first touch is. For every girl, the thrill of this special guy holding her hand can only be compared to a trip to Disney World—fireworks over Cinderella's Castle! I mean, she has an emotional heart attack; she feels electricity flow up her arm the moment he takes her hand in his. (I *still* remember where I was when Ken held my hand for the first time—Six Flags Over Georgia during our last ride together in the park before heading back to our college campus!)

Imagine in our story now that Molly has to leave Tyler because she is being picked up by her parent. So she walks away from him, giddy as a little girl on Christmas morning. She keeps saying to herself, "I can't believe he held my hand!" She's so excited she has to text ten friends on the way home in the car. Ten times she repeats her delightful experience (if you know teen girls, you *know* I am not exaggerating): "We were looking in the window at the pet store. It was *sooo* sweet! There were the cutest little puppies, and he just reached over and took my hand! Oh my gosh! I thought I was going to die!"

Now, you may be smiling at this last sentence, but, believe me, the reality of the Law of Diminishing Returns has already set in.

Let's continue the story. When Molly sees Tyler again—let's say at youth group—he holds her hand when they sit down. *This time*, even though she is happy, the fireworks over Cinderella's Castle do not happen. Molly is not "over the moon" with Tyler's hand holding hers. She is actually a bit let down. "Maybe it's because we're at youth group," she thinks. Sitting there, she is already planning how to make that amazing feeling happen again by going back to the mall. So the next week, she lies to her mom again about meeting her girlfriends at the mall, and off she goes to meet Tyler. If Tyler has encouraged Molly to lie so that they can be alone together, well, you know what group he belongs to—the *Bozo* gang! Sadly, though, girls fall for the tempting attention of Bozos because they have already marched down the list of actions that can lead to sexual sin. When it isn't thrilling enough to stare at the boy or think about him a lot, a girl will want to move to the next step and invest *more* of herself in this boy's attention. And a Bozo boy is happy to *take more!* Because you're learning quickly, I bet you know that the return on this "investment" will become less and less.

Saturday arrives and Molly's mom drops her off at the mall to meet her friends once again. When Molly spots Mr. Wonderful, he takes her hand and they begin to walk through the mall.

Within moments of Tyler holding her hand again, she is shocked. This time, when he touches her hand, there are

*When it isn't thrilling enough to stare at the boy or think about him a lot a girl will want to move to the next step and invest **more** of herself in this boy's attention.*

no fireworks, no electricity. It's not even as fun as when he took her hand at the youth meeting. She wonders, "Is this the same hand?" She even looks down at his hand as she thinks about the situation to make sure! Where did the thrill go? "Do I not like him anymore?" she thinks in a panic. "Maybe we need to walk down to the pet store where he first held my hand; maybe seeing those cute puppies will help the thrill return with the memory."

Molly leaves the mall that day *completely* puzzled by her experience. She is confused because she has no idea about the Law of Diminishing Returns. No one taught her that her disappointment with the hand holding was *predictable.* From the first time she sat at church, daydreaming about how "cute" Tyler was and repeating in her thoughts everything she had ever heard him say…she was training her mind and heart to run to this place of disappointment. What do you think Molly is going to do next? Do you think she will tell her mom what's going on and how confused she is? Do you think she'll *stop* and pray for God's wisdom? Do you think she will realize that she has set herself up by all her obsessing over Tyler?

Sadly, Molly does none of those things. The next time she and Tyler meet at the mall, she is determined to get that excited feeling back. So she actually leans herself up against him a little bit, just enough to encourage him to put his arm around her shoulders and pull her closer to his side. Guess what? The fireworks return. Phew! Molly is relieved and excited. Now she is sure that their "love" is here to stay.

This little couple's physical affection becomes a pattern. They hold hands, and at the youth meeting he sits with his arm around her. She leans against him and is so happy for this attention from her boyfriend in front of all her friends (which, by the way, their parents may not know about at all!). But do you see that these things will not keep Molly or Tyler happy for long. Because, remember this, all those thoughts and long stares move along with everything else they are doing. Now they stare into each other's eyes, and now their thoughts turn to "what comes *next*?" Molly's daydreaming isn't about how cute Tyler's dimples are; she's wondering when he will kiss her and imagining just how that will happen. It won't shock you to know that her friends are even pushing her, too. "What!? He hasn't kissed you yet?" So she is feeling pressure from the outside *as well as* from inside her body.

You could finish this story, because you know the Law of Diminishing Returns now. You can see how these teens can move along that path and do more than they ever planned to do. They don't understand that they are actually *marching* toward the No Zone with all this inappropriate physical affection that will deliver them to sexual sin.

Designed with a Purpose

If you don't understand how God made our bodies, you won't understand that when you go to the No Zone, you are going too far. That zone was made to be entered *only* in marriage. I am hoping that your mom and dad have already explained some of these principles, but I am explaining them to you, too, because you can't hear them often enough! You are in training as a Young Lady of Purity, so, just like exercising muscles to make them stronger, you are training your mind to become a strong and wise teenager! Learning about the Law of Diminishing Returns is a hugely important part of that exercise routine. You will grow your understanding "muscles" and your conviction "muscles" so that you will be prepared to make the best choices.

Sexual touching ***makes*** *people dizzy! That's why they fall into the No Zone!*

You see, even the nicest teenage girl you know, if she did the things on the list above, she could end up going further than her heart would guide her. *God created sexual affection for marriage.* God created our bodies to enjoy that affection. It was made for marriage so that a man and a woman would not need to stop and put on the brakes. In marriage, there is freedom to be who God made men and women to be together. But young people think they can play around and then miraculously find some super-human self-control once they reach the No Zone. It's like doing cartwheels on the edge of a cliff and not thinking you could fall right off—especially after you get dizzy. Sexual touching *makes* people dizzy! That's why they fall into the No Zone!

What Is It Like To Be "Treated with All Purity"?

When girls ask me what another important part of predating preparation is, I tell them that they can find it in the New Testament Book of First Timothy. It says to *"treat younger women with all purity as you would your own sisters"* (1 Timothy 5:2 NLT).

This Scripture is speaking to young guys, and it states the limits on their relationships with young women. They are to treat young women with *all* purity, as though they were siblings. So, how should a big brother treat a little sister? He should protect her, first of all. He should watch out for her and help her. Hopefully he is loving and encouraging of her. If you have read the Book of Ruth, you will recognize this behavior as a description of Boaz. Boaz responded to the virtuous behavior of Ruth and Ruth, in turn, responded with honor to him.

There is no difference in your friendships with boys now and your future dating experiences. If you learn about the *right* kind of behavior from boys and you look for that and *expect it* from them, you won't be fooled by the Bozo boys who do not treat girls with all purity. You won't be tempted to kiss a *frog* and hope he turns into a *prince!* You will wait for the prince the Lord brings along, in the Lord's timing.

If you pay attention and think about what you have been learning in this book, you will see which boys are acting like this Bible verse encourages. You will see boys who are kind and respectful to others—including other boys and teachers. You will notice which boys are always teasing or being mean and which boys can have fun but not be hurtful to others. Most important, ask the Lord in prayer to help you notice how boys honor Him. When the time comes for you to think about dating, you will know a *lot* about what "treating girls with all purity" looks like—and you will not give in to anything less than that!

Finally, I will write more about the topic of dating, especially in Chapter 10, "Becoming a Young Lady of Patience." For now, though, I want to leave you with one picture of what purity looked like for my teenaged kids. When our children were in high school, they didn't go anywhere unless they were in a group. We would joke and call it "International Date Night," because the kids were all ages and always traveled in a mob. It was like there was an "unwritten rule" they all seemed to stick to—no pairing up! What is so great is that by staying in a group and getting to know so many kids, these former teens remain friends today—and they are all in their thirties with families of their own.

Discussion Questions

Here are some questions you can think about or write about or talk about with someone else. It's not a test! So, feel free to look back in the chapter to help you think about your answers.

1. What do you think of when you heard the word "purity?"
2. How did Ruth show her purity with Boaz?
3. What does purity say about how *you* see and value yourself? Ps. 119: 9-11 and Psalm 139:14,16
4. How does purity honor God *and* respect *yourself*?
5. Explain the "Law of Diminishing Returns" and how it leads to the "No Zone."
6. What should it look like for you to be treated with *all purity*? (see 1 Timothy 5:2, NLT)

Chapter 7

Becoming a Young Lady of Security

Security flows from believing what God says about me—nothing more, nothing less. –JMK

Ruth's Security

> *Then he* [Boaz] *said, "May you be blessed of the Lord, my daughter. You have shown your last kindness to be better than the first by not going after young men, whether poor or rich. Now, my daughter, do not fear. I will do for you whatever you ask, for all my people in the city know that you are a woman of excellence"* (Ruth 3:10-11).

"A woman of excellence." Now *that* is a huge compliment! In the beginning of Chapter 6, I told you that Boaz was honored by Ruth's actions when she went to lay by his feet on the threshing floor. This is how I know—look at all that he says to her. He is impressed with Ruth's kindness toward him, because he knows that she could have gone looking for a younger man, closer to her age. He knows that she is following the Jewish practice of asking him to be her "kinsman redeemer," and by doing that she is showing her faithfulness to God. And he praises her for her great reputation in the city as a woman of virtue. Because of all that, he promises her that he will do whatever is needed to care for her.

Think about this: Ruth could not possibly have imagined that a man like Boaz would one day be her prince. He was a wealthy Israelite and she was a young Moabite—a "nobody" from a foreign land. As a young, widowed woman, Ruth must have felt lonely and wished for a husband. She could have flirted with the workers in the field or tried to catch the eye of a young man at the marketplace. But she didn't. She lived in victory over the desire to "man hunt." Instead of going after the *boys*, she sat still and let God bring her a *prince*. This is a wonderful picture of a Lady of Security. Her security—her safety, her future—she entrusted to God's timing and God's ways.

What does it mean to be "secure"? It means that you're safe and protected and that your needs are taken care of. And what does it mean to *feel* secure? To feel secure is to *know* and to *have confidence* in the fact that you are secure. It means that you don't spend time worrying about what's going to happen to you; you are at peace that you will be cared for. Can you even imagine that there are Christians who live in places where they have famines and terrible poverty who *still feel secure?* My son, Ben, went on a trip to Africa when he was a teenager, and he was blown away by the *security* that some very poor people showed by their amazing joy and peace. They didn't always know where the next meal was coming from, but they were secure that God loves them, even in the difficult trials of this life. So, the reality is that being secure does not depend on how much money someone has. It doesn't depend on perfect health. It is a strength and peace that God is in charge of your life.

By the time you are nine or ten years old, you have probably learned the word *insecurity*. This, of course, is the opposite of feeling secure—it is a deep feeling of nervousness or fear that tempts us with all kinds of worry-thoughts. Our mind can be flooded with worry-thoughts about a BFF: "Does she like me? Does she hate me? Oh no! She didn't message me back right away—she must be mad at me!" What about this kind of worry: "Does this dress look good on me? Maybe they'll think it's ugly. What if someone else has the same dress? I'll be *so* embarrassed!" Or, you might know these sort of thoughts: "I can't get up in front of the class for this project. I'll look stupid! I'll sound dumb. Hannah is so much smarter than I am—I can't go right after her!"

Being secure does not depend on how much money someone has. It doesn't depend on perfect health. It is a strength and peace that God is in charge of your life.

These kinds of thoughts and the feelings that go with them are "insecurity." I hope you know that everyone struggles with one kind of insecurity or another, even when people pretend that they don't. I also hope you know that Jesus wants to heal us from insecurity, because He died to give us *security!* He gave up His life so that we could give up our self-centered sins that tempt us with a *fake security.* Do you know what I mean by that term fake (or false) security? Think about that last set of nervous thoughts I wrote above—the ones about giving a report in front of class. Read them over again. Can you see that it's like the worry itself is a gremlin that jumps right up on you and yells in your ear, "I'll keep you safe! If you keep imagining all the terrible things that could happen to you, you'll stay *safe!* But if you stop worrying, you'll die!" So you keep up the insecure worry, and before you know it you are completely frozen in your seat, unable to stand up or walk or speak! Talk about a bunch of lies! The worry promises to protect you...but you end up feeling more foolish than ever!

Back in Chapter 5, "Becoming a Young Lady of Devotion," we looked at the Kingdom of Self and how being "me-centered" is a rotten way to live. It's the same thing with insecurity—it's no way to live, it makes you miserable, and it does not serve God. It's a way of being me-centered, because when I'm insecure, all the focus is on...*me!* This is also called being "self-conscious," when lots of thought and attention is on *self!* Let's go back to Ruth's story and learn something about a young woman who did not give in to self-conscious insecurity.

Hiding One's Insecurities under His Wings

As you know, Ruth faced the difficulties of a young widow in a foreign land. More than just being in a foreign land, she was from a nation that Israel hated. In fact, the men who described her to Boaz didn't call her "Ruth" or even "Naomi's daughter-in-law" or "Mahlon's widow." They called her "the Moabite," and I can almost hear their voices as they sneered at her. Think of it like this: Does your town or school have a rival team that they play the biggest game of the year against? Does your family cheer for a certain football team, like the Miami Dolphins? Well, Ruth showing up to glean in the fields would be like you walking into the rival team's stands wearing your team's tee shirt and hat, like a Pittsburgh Steelers fan, all decked out in black and gold, going over to sit on the Miami side of the stands at the Dolphins' own stadium. Those Miami fans would yell "*Boo!*" and other insults at the Steelers fan. They would yell at him to "*Go home*" and maybe even throw some paper cups at him! It would not be a delightful experience, to say the least. Now realize that Ruth's experience would be much worse than that—*and* she had to face it every day in this new place she came to.

Now, Ruth certainly couldn't change her situation or her nationality as a Moabite. So how did she face the hatred and disgust she knew she was going to face? How did she have the courage and *security* to go to the fields, when she could be sure that some people would be really mean to her and others totally ignore her? The answer you well know. *She could rest in the true God she had come to trust.* Her insecurity was overcome by security in her relationship with God. Ruth hid her insecurities under the wings of the Almighty.

> *Have mercy on me, O God, have mercy on me, for in you I take refuge. I will take refuge in the shadow of your wings until the disaster has passed* (Psalm 57:1 NIV).

Have you learned to take your insecurities to God and rest in the shadow of His wings? Would those closest to you know that your security is in God, that you hide—or "take refuge," as the Psalm says—in Him? When Boaz had one of his first conversations with Ruth, he spoke about her security, resting under the covering of God's wings. He *saw* her acting in ways that could only come from her security in the Lord. Boaz was fully aware that Ruth had every reason to be insecure, being both a Moabite and a young widow. Encouraging her, he made the most wonderful remark about the security she clearly had in God:

> *May the Lord repay you for what you have done. May you be richly rewarded by the Lord, the God of Israel, under whose wings you have come to take refuge* (Ruth 2:12 NIV).

Ruth's insecurity was overcome by security in her relationship with God.

You Are Fearfully and Wonderfully Made!

As you are growing up, you have a lot of role models around you—your mom and grandmothers, maybe an aunt or two, a big sister, teachers and ladies at church, your friends' moms. Those ladies can be examples of the security they find in the Lord, or they can model insecurity. Some women have learned to believe that people will like them or dislike them depending totally on how they look. Maybe, when she was your age, some kids teased a lady about her curly red hair and freckles—and for the rest of her life she has felt ugly and insecure about her hair and skin. What's so sad about this is that I could see that woman and exclaim, "Wow! What gorgeous hair you have! I *love* red hair!" and she would not even be able to really hear that compliment, because her insecurity is screaming in her head, "Not *my* hair! *My* hair is a hideous mess of curls!" As another example, my mom was always worried about her weight and often made comments about other women and their weight. Unfortunately, I grew up with this same self-focused insecurity and have battled this unhealthy body image for far too much of my life. But do you know what the Lord has taught me? That He made me and that I am a wonderful work of His creation. Here it is, right in His Word:

> *For you created my inmost being; you knit me together in my mother's womb.*
>
> *I praise you because I am fearfully and wonderfully made; your works are wonderful, I know that full well.*

My frame was not hidden from you when I was made in the secret place, when I was woven together in the depths of the earth (Psalm 139:13-15 NIV).

What does this Psalm tell us? That whether you are tall or short, whether you have freckles or thin or thick hair, whether you have brown eyes or green eyes, your heavenly Father made you that way. Therefore, you can be fully blessed in it because you are fully loved by Him. If we allow some physical part of ourselves to say how valuable we are, no wonder we get insecure and forget how fearfully and wonderfully made we are.

Women and even girls spend countless hours looking in the mirror every week—fixing our hair or picking out the perfect outfit…covering our freckles, highlighting our eyelids with makeup, or extending our lashes. We want to be *noticed, admired, and loved.* As females created in the image of God, our longing for such love is natural. Also, it's not a bad thing to want to look our best and look nice. I believe it's actually a good thing to desire the right kinds of approval. For example, to dress up in special clothes for church or a party is a way of joining in the celebration and respecting your hosts. To make your hair look nice and put on clean and pretty outfits for school is also respectful to the school community. But sinful human nature has twisted this need and made it a very selfish thing.

Even if you haven't learned from the women you know personally to be self-conscious about how you look, there is a billion-dollar business that *surrounds* us and helps tempt girls and their moms to be insecure about their bodies. TV shows, commercials, movies, magazines, video games, pop singers—the girls and women in these pictures are made to look like "someone's" idea of perfect. They have bright white, perfectly straight teeth. Their hair is styled in the latest fashion, without one hair out of place. Their clothes are hip; their hips are thin—can you say "Barbie Doll"?! Sometimes these girls look more like robots or anime characters than any kind of *real* person. *But*, if you and your girlfriends compare yourselves to those pictures, your self-image can still suffer—even if you know those pictures have been Photoshopped and the actresses on the screens have been spray tanned!

Insecurity and an Empty Love Tank

I want to draw you a word picture to help explain one way people get insecure. Have you ever been in the car with your parents and it ran out of gas? I hope not, because that is never a fun experience. But I want you to imagine the scene…the tank gets low on gas and the car starts to "chug, chug, chug" and it jerks back and forth with almost no gas getting into the engine. Then it just slows all the way down to a stop. It's empty. Nothing the driver can do can start it again until someone pours more gas into it. You can also imagine in this situation that things are pretty tense. The driver might be really mad or scared, and probably no one in the car is very happy.

Keep that story in mind and now think about our hearts as if they're gas tanks. Our hearts are the tanks and *love* is the gasoline that makes them run. A full tank is the best. On a full tank, you can drive far and not worry about running out of gas. But a tank that's low on love makes someone nervous or cranky or sad—like the car sputtering. A *really* sad person may feel like her love tank is completely empty, like she's stranded on the side of the road. It's not a good state to be in, and most people try to find ways to fill up that tank.

The best way to fill up your love tank is to go to God in prayer and tell Him how it feels. His Love Letter to you, His Bible, is overflowing with gas for your love tank! It's also great to tell someone, like your mom or dad, that you need some extra love and get a big hug and some encouraging words. Everyone's love tank feels like it's running low sometimes, and to ask for a "fill-up" is a truly wise thing to do.

Our hearts are the tanks and love is the gasoline that makes them run.

However, for girls especially, if her father has not been around much while she's growing up, or if he's not such a loving man, then her love tank may not be as full as it needs to be. Why do I say "for girls especially"? Because if girls don't have daddies to help fill their love tanks, they often look to *boys* to do that. They look to a boy to do a man's work. This is most unfortunate, because no boy or teen guy can replace the kind of love a girl needs from her dad.

Such an empty love tank needs *supernatural* filling by our heavenly Father. A Young Lady of Security can become secure in Jesus as He fills her heart—and He can use other wise, caring people to help do that. It is not surprising that many of my daughter's friends did not have fathers in their lives. Whenever I could, I would encourage these fatherless girls to go home and look online on a Bible search site and search for all the verses that talk about God as Father. Fatherless girls can definitely have their love tanks filled as they learn the reality of God as Father.

> *And do not call anyone on earth "father," for you have one Father, and he is in heaven* (Matthew 23:9 NIV).

Papa God can fill the hole left by a father who left his family or a father who has his own empty love tank and doesn't seem to have much love to give. As you grow to understand the love of God as Father, your heart's love tank will not only fill up, but it won't empty out the way it once did. This is so important, because guess what kind of boys go after a girl who feels empty? It's Bozo boys who seem to know what girls to go after—girls who are empty and ache for male attention and affection. If you have a girlfriend who already seems "boy crazy," or if you know a teen girl who seems to be obsessed with boys, it is often because her love tank has not been filled at home. This is even more common if a girl comes from a divorced home.

If you are in this situation right now, I want to encourage you—every night before you close your eyes, pray, "Oh Jesus, fill my love tank."

When I was just a young teenager, I already had a pretty empty love tank. As a new Christian reading the Bible for the first time, I came across the Scripture I shared above, Matthew 23:9, *"Do not call anyone on earth 'father,' for you have one Father, and he is in heaven"* (NIV). With childlike faith I claimed God as my only true Father. And now 47 years later, I can still remember declaring, "I claim You, Father God, as *my* Papa." Still living in very troubled home, I would constantly remind myself of the love of my heavenly Papa.

> *Praise be to the God and Father of our Lord Jesus Christ, the Father of compassion and the God of all comfort* (2 Corinthians 1:3 NIV).

Father God so filled my love tank that I was able to wait for God's *best* rather than settle for a Bozo. Secure in God, I waited for my Boaz, whom I've now had for 40 years. So my love tank was filled to overflowing by my Father God.

Oh God, Keep an Eye on Her

One more thing about Papa God I want to share with you. This is a wonderful promise for all God's girls. Whether you have a wonderful relationship with your father or you live with the pain of his absence, this verse can be a security-building promise of hope:

...I am coming to you. Holy Father, protect them by the power of your name... (John 17:11 NIV).

In this verse, Jesus Christ Himself prayed for you—yes, you! He did it before He left earth. He asked the Father to guard not only you, but all those who will come to know Him in the future.

In John 17:11, the word *protect* means "to guard" or "keep an eye." Jesus, in the garden almost 2,000 years ago, asked God Almighty to keep an eye on you. This is so awesome! It's a promise from Jesus that you can pray as well. And when you are asking God to keep an eye on you, you are praying in perfect harmony with God's heart.

Maybe we need to think about this just a little longer. Before Jesus left the earth, in His last prayer, He asked Papa God to guard and protect you. Now, that should have you on your feet cheering and doing a happy dance. That thought should be the foundation of your security—the rock you can stand on. God is keeping an eye on you, and that is your *ultimate* security. You can walk through the halls at school with a smile on your face just thinking, "The God of the Universe has got me covered!" Along with your cry for Father God to fill you love tank, you can add *praise* for the fact that God is keeping an eye on you.

God's unfailing love for us is a fact stated over and over in the Scriptures. It is true whether we completely understand it or even believe it or not. *Our* doubts do not destroy God's love. And *our* faith does not create God's love. So we can't destroy that love. It begins in the very heart of God, because God *is* love. It flows to us through our relationship with His beloved Son.

You can grow stronger as a Young Lady of Security just thinking about God keeping an eye on you.

Screaming the Truth

> Insecurity among women (young and old) is epidemic, but it is not incurable. Don't expect it to go away quietly, however. We're going to have to let truth scream louder to our souls than the lies that have infected us.[1]

I love this quote by Beth Moore, because it tells us that insecurity is like a sickness all around us. It's an epidemic! The germs that cause that sickness are *lies*. However, there is a cure, and that cure comes from our choices to *speak the truth!* The Devil is the "father of lies" (see John 8:44), and he screams lies at our hearts daily. He is like that gremlin of worry I described earlier. In Jesus, we are given the power to scream back at him to *go away*, but we can only scream back if our hearts are filled with the truth (see John 8:32). You and I need to learn how to *scream* at the *liar!* It may seem strange for a Young Lady of Security to be screaming—but girls, there really are times when we need to.

When I was a young Christian, I would often have thoughts that I was completely worthless. I too often saw myself as damaged, broken, and no good to anyone. I can't remember exactly when I first began to scream back at the enemy of my soul. But I definitely remember one time when I was walking to my car after sharing my heart with some teen girls, and as I was backing my car out of the church parking lot, I had this thought: "If those girls knew what a loser you really are, they would never listen to you!"

I can still remember how quickly tears came to my eyes and how quickly the thoughts of being a loser poured into my heart. *Yet,* as quickly as this attack of insecurity invaded my soul, I remembered a verse that I had just learned, Revelation 12:10-11:

> For the accuser of our brothers and sisters, who accuses them before our God day and night, has been hurled down. They triumphed over him by the blood of the Lamb and by the word of their testimony… (NIV).

As I thought about the lying "accuser" (one who blames others) of all Christians, right there in my car I—as boldly as a teenager could—screamed, "You can go back to where you belong, because I belong to Jesus and His blood is my confidence!"

That screaming moment in my car became an example for the many times in the future when I would experience these kinds of accusing thoughts and would overcome the liar with the scream of truth! Even if my "scream" sometimes has to be a whisper, I have learned to speak the truth against those lies.

Secure Enough to Face Bullies and Mean Girls

When our daughter was a teenager, God signed us up for some pretty challenging "classes." These classes had lessons about mean girls and bullying boys. I have to say that I am actually grateful for the "classes I took" about mean kids. Now, you know I didn't really go to school to learn these things—but sometimes it sure felt like it, because I had to study and do my homework to understand what Jesus wanted us to do. It was often painful, but Jessi and I learned so much about jealousy and how destructive it is.

Most importantly, we also learned a lot about forgiving the emotional bullies, Bozo boys, and mean girls she sometimes faced. If I, as a Christian mom, had not been committed to forgiving others, I might have ended up in the news—you would have heard about a furious, screaming mom who was going crazy on teen girls who were so hurtful to others without a cause! Phew! The love of Jesus saved me from getting arrested—ha!

During mean-girl and mocking Bozo-boy encounters, I knew that our daughter needed to develop a most important ability. This ability can bring good out of evil and transform such difficult trials into a mission field! Because you are growing as a Young Lady of both Faith and Diligence, I bet you can guess what I am going to say: I taught our daughter how to overcome evil with good by *praying* for the mean girls and mocking boys and asking God to transform their sad, mean hearts. Seeing God's healing and changing work in the middle of hurtful bullying experiences will help you grow as a Young Lady of Security.

One sample of what these mean girls did was to write nasty words under some pictures of Jessi. Her picture was shown with other kids in the school who won awards. And you know what they were mocking her for winning? Awards for Best School Spirit and Class Spiritual Leader! So Jessi was mocked because of her joyful love for her school and her Lord. What on earth would make kids be mean about such wonderful qualities? Well, these bullies were *jealous* of Jessi, which means they were at war with the good in her. She and I prayed and asked the Lord to help us forgive those jealous acts that hurt and embarrassed Jessi...and I need to report to you that, years later, those girls came and confessed what they had done. So, the Lord rewarded us with the gift of their confession, and rewarded them with knowing they were forgiven.

It is my true wish that no one reading this book has been hurt by bullying. But, sadly, I know that's not likely. I know that bullying can begin so early in kids' lives—sometimes even in pre-school or kindergarten! Once in a while, the bullies are even from a girl's own family. Here is a hugely important thing to learn, though: These kids who are mean to others are not *secure* enough to love others...their insecurity makes them think they are at war with the good in other children! They have their own "gremlin thoughts" that jump up and yell at them and tell them that if they're mean, they are strong. It's a *big bunch of lies*, but it's such a tempting *false security* (remember how I describe those earlier in this chapter?). It is my heart's passion to encourage God's girls everywhere, so they can make good choices in a world where bad choices are too common. Also, though, I want *you* to be wise and be able to face jealous cruelty with the truth of who you are in God's eyes. Or, God may put you in the role of encouraging a friend or a sibling who is facing such battling bullies.

With God for Me, Who Could Be Against Me?

If you have ever been made fun of or if anyone has ever been so critical of you that the pain knocked the breath right out of you, you and I have something in common. When I was a girl, I lived in a home where criticism and mean teasing happened so often, it was like someone had written it in on the daily schedule! One day, though, a godly woman I talked to said to me, "Whenever you are criticized, think about *who* is speaking and that will help you with your reaction." Because, whoever it was, it wasn't

Jesus! So, that began to help change how I heard those words that could be very cruel.

Now I have learned that whenever I am criticized, I first ask the Lord to show me anything that may be truth, so that I can repent and let Jesus change me in that area. When the criticism goes against something that Jesus says about me, I choose to believe Jesus rather than another person. Whatever people say about me, I listen to; but I bring the comments to Jesus and compare them to what the Bible tells me about His love for me. *God's* opinion of me is where I live, rest, and have confidence. How do I know what God's opinion of me is? Well, His Love Letter to us is full of truth about who we are to Him. Here is a sample of how Jesus would describe one of His girls:

- She is chosen and dearly loved by *Me* (see 1 Thessalonians 1:4; Colossians 3:12).
- She is a child of *Mine*, part of *My* family (see Romans 8:15-16).
- She is free to call *Me* "Daddy" (see Galatians 4:6).
- She was on *My* mind before I spoke the world into existence (see 2 Timothy 1:9).
- She is a one of a kind, custom designed by *Me* (see Ephesians 2:10).

- She is getting better with every passing moment (see 2 Corinthians 5:17).
- She is part of a royal calling and responsibility (see 1 Peter 2:9-10).
- She is an heir of an unshakable Kingdom (see Galatians 4:6-7; Hebrews 12:28).
- She is aware of her enemy, but is without fear (see 1 Peter 5:8).

The next time someone speaks to you in a mean or critical way, just pause and pray, "Oh, Papa God! My security comes from what *You* say about me!"

Why do we even let people's rejection of us (or when we think they are rejecting us) control us more than the acceptance we have received from God Almighty through Jesus?

> *In face of all this, what is there left to say? If God is for us, who can be against us?* (Romans 8:31 PNT)

Clean Out Your Closet

As I said, the reality in life is that everyone has some kind of insecurity. I like to say that if a person is *breathing* she will struggle with insecurity from time to time—so, if you're breathing today, welcome to the club! No matter how much a girl is loved by parents and siblings, there are things that will cause her to worry and feel like her security is being attacked. Yet, hopefully, in the love of Jesus, we are all growing out of these insecurities the same way we grow out of jackets and shoes. We grow out of them and get to just throw them away—not even donate them to the thrift-store! How do you know what to throw away? Well, first, you need to go through your closet and take a good look at what you actually have in there. The same way, you can pray to God and ask for help taking a good look at what makes you worry or feel insecure. You can ask your mom or dad or another trusted person to help you think about these things, too. That way, you can notice, for example, that when you get around certain kids at school or at church, you feel nervous, and those worry-thoughts tend to creep up on you.

Next, a great idea is to make a list in your journal of these fears and worries and then you *and* your parents can be praying for the Holy Spirit to remind you of some of the skills I have shared with you in this chapter: Remembering that God is watching over you and asking Him to fill up your love tank; "screaming" away the devil's lies and repeating the truths of how *Jesus* describes you. After doing this for a time, you will start to see that those worries are getting old and worn out. Day by day, you will come to see that you don't need that insecurity any more—and you can throw it right out with the trash!

You can pray to God and ask for help taking a good look at what makes you worry or feel insecure.

In the rest of this chapter, I am going to share with you two lists that will help you as you work to clean out your closet of insecurities. Don't let the first list overwhelm you, because the second one is the answer to the first. But showing you this list might really help you think about what makes *you* feel insecure, *and* it will remind you that you are *not alone* in this process. The first list shows you the answers that 12- to 15-year-old girls gave in interviews. The girls were asked to share the things they worried about the most—just like I suggested you do. I am certain you will see some things that sound very familiar to you:

1. Girls talking about me
2. What other people think about whatever I'm doing
3. If my friends are really going to be my friends when other people are around
4. If I get in a fight with my friends, are we going to hate each other and become rivals?
5. Grades
6. Boys
7. Friend who is being mean
8. Rumors about me
9. Doing well in school and in other areas of life
10. Trying to be good at everything
11. Trying to make myself worth someone's time

12. Fighting with siblings
13. Loneliness
14. Messing up my life and not realizing it
15. That people will think I'm weird
16. Not making the right choices
17. Gaining weight
18. If people judge me from how I look
19. That I won't know how to get out of a bad situation
20. Getting into trouble

These answers show the kinds of self-conscious fears that pretty much all kids have at least some of. Do you see that they all have to do with what others think of you and how you think about yourself? And can you think what the best cure is for getting so nervous about these things? What is the fastest exit from the Kingdom of Self? Exactly! We need to keep learning and practicing the *truth of what God thinks of us!*

Some Security Boosters!

Now, here is the second list I promised you. *This* list is made up of the good news of God's loving power that is infinitely stronger than the bad news of worry and insecurity. Ask your mom for a set of index cards or choose a special little notebook. You can copy the list below if you have a printer at home and then cut out each truth and glue it to a card or a page in the notebook. If you love to write things out—you can do that, instead. Then, keep your set of "Truths" on the nightstand by your bed. You will be blessed by having these truths close by. They will be right there for you to look at before going to sleep at night or when you wake up in the morning.

After a long day, these cards will be a refreshing reminder of the truth about you. Security must come from a good self-image that reflects what *God says about you*—nothing more and nothing less.

Eleven Truths to Strengthen Security and Fight Insecurity

> *We...are being transformed into the same image from glory to glory, just as from the Lord, the Spirit* (2 Corinthians 3:18).

Truth #1–Do Not Think of Myself Negatively.

If I am hard on myself, I am likely to be hard on others.

...Love your neighbor as yourself (Matthew 22:39).

Truth #2–Behave with God-Confidence.

God-confidence is the opposite of arrogance and pride.

For the Spirit God gave us does not make us timid, but gives us power, love and self-discipline (2 Timothy 1:7 NIV).

Truth #3–When I Fail, Confess, and Refuse to Condemn Myself.

If I fail, it only means I am human—everyone fails!

If we confess our sins, he is faithful and just and ***will forgive*** *us our sins…* (1 John 1:9 NIV).

There is now no condemnation for those who are in Christ Jesus (Romans 8:1 NIV).

Truth #4–Do Not Compare Myself with Others.

Comparisons actually break down my spirit.

I am unique, one of a kind; I am fearfully and wonderfully made, therefore I am incomparable.

When they measure themselves by themselves and compare themselves with themselves, they are not wise (2 Corinthians 10:12 NIV).

Truth #5–Concentrate on God's Grace.

A definition of grace: to bow down in order to benefit another/others greatly. *God* has done this for me!

God's grace is strength given to me to help behave myself.

See what great the love the Father has lavished on us, that we should be called children of God! And that is what we are! (1 John 3:1 NIV)

Truth #6–Spend Time and Make Friends with Positive People.

As I befriend, I become. My closest friends are an image of the future me!

Walk with the wise and become wise… (Proverbs 13:20 NIV).

Truth #7–Learn How to Rejoice in All Things.

The key to emotional health is being thankful and grateful.

Give thanks in all circumstances; for this is God's will for you in Christ Jesus (1 Thessalonians 5:18 NIV).

Truth #8–Have Realistic Expectations of Myself and Others.

Remember, on my best day…I am still "dust" (see Psalm 103:13-14).

What I expect from someone today may be my disappointment tomorrow.

...Do not think of yourself more highly than you ought, but rather think of yourself with sober judgment... (Romans 12:3 NIV).

Truth #9—Growth and Change Are a Process, and Never Happen in an Instant.

God is the One who makes the changes in me (see John 17:17).

The start is the promise of the finish (see Philippians 1:6; 1 Thessalonians 5:24).

In God's corrections, He never stops believing in me!

For whom the Lord loves He reproves, even as a father corrects the son in whom he delights (Proverbs 3:12).

Truth #10—Do What Is Right and Pleasing to Jesus.

Pleasing Jesus is not the same as pleasing people (see Matthew 6:1).

If I were still trying to please people, I would not be a servant of Christ (Galatians 1:10 NIV).

Truth #11—Be Positive.

I can "fast" from critical words. The Holy Spirit can help me stop thinking them and speaking them.

I can pray for a "mouth filter" to filter what I am tempted to say:

> *Finally, brothers and sisters, whatever is true, whatever is noble, whatever is right, whatever is pure, whatever is lovely, whatever is admirable—if anything is excellent or praiseworthy—**think about such things*** (Philippians 4:8 NIV).

As you practice and think about these *most important* truths, you will be changed by God from the inside out. You will know more and more who you are in *His* eyes, how *He* created you; and you will become a stronger and stronger Young Lady of Security.

Note

1. Beth Moore, *So Long Insecurity: You've Been a Bad Friend to Us* (Carol Stream, IL: Tyndale House Publishers, 2010), xiii.

Discussion Questions

Here are some questions you can think about or write about or talk about with someone else. It's not a test! So, feel free to look back in the chapter to help you think about your answers.

1. Where was Ruth's source of security and how did this protect her from making poor choices?
2. What does it mean for you to be and *feel* secure? Psalm 139:14,16
3. Ask God to show you some insecurities that you need to give over to Him. Then pray something like:

   Father, my security and my trust are in You. I will not fear because You are with me.

   The Bible says that if You are for me, no one can be against me. Right now, I give all of my insecurities over to You. [now, list things that you are insecure, fearful or are worrying about...don't hold back, God already knows what's going on!]

   I give these to You, Lord and I ask you to keep them. Help me not to try and take them back. Replace thoughts of worry, insecurity and fear with what Your Word says about Who You are and who I am. Help me to believe what You say about me, no matter what anybody else says. I am secure and confident in Christ!

   In Jesus' Name, Amen!

4. How can insecurity influence who you end up being attracted to and dating?

5. What does it mean to "Scream the Truth?"

6. Think about some of the lies you believe. Maybe they sound like,

    "You're worthless."

    "You've gone too far...you've messed up too much. No one will ever love you."

    "You'll never be perfect like..." (and name the person you are always comparing yourself to)

    "You're not cool like..." (name the cool person)

Lies come in all shapes and sizes. They also tend to be custom made to fit your insecurity.

This is why it's so important for you to know what the Bible says about who you are. The Bible is not just an old book filled with "Dos" and "Don'ts." That's a lie in and of itself! The Word of God actually says who you are and most importantly, what God says about you! Spend some time in the Bible today and ask the Lord to tell you what *He* thinks about you. You'll be amazed!

And if you need some help getting started, go back to page 163 and review how Jesus would describe one of His precious girls. *This* is how He sees you!

You can also go to pages 168–171 for *Eleven Truths to Strengthen Security and Fight Insecurity.* I would write some of these down and memorize them. Keep them in front of you!

Chapter 8

Becoming a Young Lady of Contentment

Nothing is more beautiful than a content woman. –JMK

"*Waaah! Waaah!*" Can you "hear" what I'm writing? That's the sound of a baby crying—not just whimpering, but screaming! What would she be saying if she had words? "I'm hungry! I'm wet! Someone woke me up!" That little one is definitely *not* at peace, wouldn't you agree? While she's fussing and crying, she's the exact image of what it is to be "discontent." She wants, wants, wants—and what she wants, she wants *now!*

"*Aaah…aaah…*" What's that sound? Well, as best as I can put it into print, it's the sound of a nice, long, satisfied sigh. Try saying it aloud with a big breath out; it's a calming noise to make, isn't it? And because we were just "listening" to the baby screaming, I feel better already. "*Aaaah…*" would be the opposite of "*Waaah!*" It's a sound of peace and *contentment*, when everything is just fine and there is no worry.

(I picture Mommy saying "*Aaah*..." once baby got cared for and settled down.)

Do you notice something about those two words? They are just one letter different! Take away the *w* in *waaah* and you have the word *aaah*. I know they don't exactly rhyme, but how cool is that! Take away a letter and you completely change the mood. Let's see in this chapter if we can learn something about contentment so that we can just "change one letter" in our hearts to go from being *discontent* to *content*.

Ruth's Contentment

If you think again about Ruth's life, people would say she had the perfect excuse to be discontent. That sweet young woman lost her husband after only ten years of marriage. Along with the grief, this experience could certainly fill someone with self-pity and bitterness. Yet, what do you know about Ruth? Ruth chose to hold tightly to the God of Israel, whom she found to be trustworthy even in great difficulties. Then, as she faced each day's task with contentment, Ruth was given the attention of the most eligible bachelor in town.

In Chapter 10, you'll read about another wonderful quality, *patience*; but I want to make a note here so that you can see that *contentment* and *patience* share something important in common. They both have to do with *waiting*. We need to be patient to wait for something, and a true sign of that patience is contentment. The Bible tells us that Ruth's mother-in-law encouraged her to be patient as she faithfully obeyed what God was calling her to do, and because of this I am sure that she was also content.

> *Then Naomi said, "Wait, my daughter, until you find out what happens. For the man will not rest until the matter is settled today"* (Ruth 3:18 NIV).

Naomi did not want Ruth's heart to race ahead into disappointment in case things did not go as they hoped. Naomi knew that instructing Ruth to "wait" was not meant to cause Ruth suffering; instead, her wise advice was meant to prevent suffering. We can experience so much needless pain when we run ahead of God's plan. Contentment comes when we choose to be patient and trust God for His perfect plan.

Discontentment Overshadows Joy

So, what is it that makes us not be content? When we find ourselves discontent, we are all too often focusing on what is missing from our lives rather than seeing what is going well with our lives. Ruth could have kept her mind only on the sadness of being a young widow. She could have talked to people about how unfair it was and complained that she didn't "deserve" such a tragedy. She could have walked about Bethlehem in a constant, self-focused,

When we find ourselves discontent, we are all too often focusing on what is missing from our lives rather than seeing what is going well with our lives.

mourning state. But this is not the picture we are given in Scripture. Ruth trusted God with her circumstances and went to work in the barley harvest rather than practicing all kinds of "poor me" thoughts.

If you think about where "poor me" thoughts come from, we wouldn't have them if we weren't comparing ourselves with someone else. A child in Haiti may not even know about iPads, so it's unlikely he's thinking, "Poor me, I don't have the newest iPad." He *may* struggle with thoughts that he doesn't have his own soccer ball, but there are no kids around him with iPads to compare himself to. Comparing one's life with others' lives can be a dangerous activity. We can become terribly discontent when we compare our lives in negative ways. Now, *if* someone (like the little Haitian boy) has a godly attitude and compares his situation with someone else, it may go like this: "Wow. My friend is so blessed to have his own soccer ball. I'm really happy for him. And what a great guy he is to bless us *all* by sharing it!" Sadly though, many people tend to compare negatively, thinking out of selfishness. Such negative comparing will always block out joy. Like dark clouds covering the sun, it will cast a dark shadow on the light of joy.

Paul the apostle warned us about this discontentment that comes from foolish comparisons:

> *For who do you know that really knows you, knows your heart? And even if they did, is there anything they would discover in you that you could take credit for? Isn't*

*everything you **have** and everything you **are** sheer gifts from God? So what's the point of all this comparing and competing?* (1 Corinthians 4:7 MSG)

Paul is saying that because God knows us, has made us, and gives each of us what we have, comparing with one another is dangerous. Such comparisons completely ignore *God's* will in our lives. In fact, in the verse right before this one, Paul tells them they are being prideful in their comparing. *Pride*, you see, is the basis of self-pity. Pride tells us that we "deserve" something, and if we don't get what we want, that angry pride can turn right into self-pity. And self-pity is the biggest enemy of contentment, peace, and joy.

Too many girls think they are joyless because they are "boyfriend-less." Or they are discontent because they do not have a "BFF" right now. Perhaps one girl lives in a big house and gets lots of new clothes while another shares a small apartment with a large family and gets hand-me-down clothes. She thinks this is "*unfair*," and she is grumpy and miserable. The unfortunate fact for anyone with this mindset is that they are joyless because they are not content with God's will for their lives.

Ask Jesus to help you see anything in your heart you feel self-pity or discontent over, anywhere you might be comparing yourself to others negatively. If you have written in your journal some of the insecurities you want to pull out of your closet (from Chapter 7), you should take a look at that list. You will see that insecurity and discontentment have a lot in common. They both come from comparing your life with your ideas about someone else's life! Here's an example: If you feel insecure about a really smart girl in your class and you worry that other people think you're not so smart, then all that worry leaves you feeling unhappy and very discontent. You have compared yourself to her and come up with a negative picture of both of you. *But* what if you chose to pray for that girl? What if you *thanked God* for how clever that girl is and looked for a chance to say a kind word to her? Such generous and kind thoughts about another person will soften your heart, and you will see that insecurity will melt away while contentment will bloom.

Contentment and Holy Sweat

If Ruth had been full of pride and discontented self-pity, she would never have volunteered to work in the hot sun in a barley field. Discontentment would have kept her at home pouting about her life. But think of this: If she had done that, she would have missed God's provision of food for her and Naomi, *and* she also would have missed the divine appointment of meeting her prince.

> *And Ruth the Moabitess said to Naomi, "Please let me go to the field and glean among the ears of grain after one in whose sight I may find favor." And she said to her, "Go, my daughter"* (Ruth 2:2).

Notice that Ruth said, *"Let* me go to the field and glean." Ruth was asking for the chance to meet not only her own need but also Naomi's needs. Ruth's contentment allowed her to do something hard for a greater good. And what's great is that she had *no idea* what would come of her contented choice. She had no idea that God would reward her obedience to Him in such abundant ways. Serving others, though, is a perfect escape out of the Kingdom of Self. It delivers one from self-pity and will grow one's contentment. Here is a quote from another book, where the author explains this beautifully:

> Doing nothing for others is the undoing of one's self. We must be purposely kind and generous, or we miss the best part of existence. The heart that goes out of itself gets large and full of joy. This is the secret of the inner life. We do ourselves the most good doing something for others....[1]

If you are struggling and tempted to feel sorry for yourself, ask the Lord to show you something you can do for someone else. Doing for others will not only help you develop as a Young Lady of Contentment, it will also boost your growth as a Young Lady of Diligence. As the Bible says, *"Godliness with contentment is great gain"* (1 Timothy 6:6 NIV).

Discontentment and Boredom

I'll tell you another mindset that can lead to discontentment—being bored. When my kids would tell me they were bored, I would ask each of them to think of something they could do for someone else. You see, contentment, like any other good attitude, is something we have to practice and learn. Life gives us many chances to "learn contentment." As a mom, I tried to be a great coach in teaching my kids to grow in contentment. When they would think of something to do for someone else, like call their grandparents just to say "Hi" or make a card to cheer up a friend or offer to help one another with a project, I would cheer them on to do it! My goal was to cheer both my kids *out* of boredom and *into* contentment and joy.

> ...*whoever refreshes others will be refreshed* (Proverbs 11:25 NIV).

Discontentment and Loneliness

Learning to be content when you are bored is important. Likewise, learning to be content when you are "alone" is a great skill. Some people develop this skill because of their God-given personalities—you might know someone (or be someone) who is at peace and happy when she is all alone for a while. You may love to sit quietly and read for a long time or happily work doing a creative project. For others of us, though, we have to pay attention and learn how to be peaceful when we are on our own. We must learn how to be "alone" without being "lonely." Being alone without being lonely means that we need to understand that *at this very moment* God knows what is going on in our lives. He has planned for *this very moment* in His design for our lives. Most importantly, we must understand that we are never really alone! As Christians, the Holy Spirit lives in our hearts, and Jesus is with us *every* moment.

> *Lord, you alone are my portion and my cup; you make my lot secure* (Psalm 16:5 NIV).

An afternoon with no plans with a friend is not a mistake by a loving God. Discontentment, however, grows by focusing on someone else's "portion," like knowing that some other friends do have plans together or your sibling is having a friend over, while you are wandering around your home with no plans and no one to share your time with.

We must learn how to be "alone" without being "lonely."

Girls, it's so good to understand that our loneliness can't always be fixed, but it can *always be accepted* as the will of God *for now;* such acceptance turns loneliness into something beautiful. I watched this reality up close and personal while our daughter spent many Friday nights alone, but not lonely. She learned the discipline of trusting God with time alone.

This ability to be content alone turned out to be very helpful in our daughter's future. When she went off to a college where she didn't know anyone and then transferred to another college also without friends there, I knew deep in my heart that her ability to be patient as she made new friends was developed in high school on those Friday nights at home. In the journey God has *you* on, this skill is a wonderful heart guard. To be content when you're on your own means that you won't be tempted to spend time with kids who are trouble-makers—like Bozo boys and mean girls. You won't be desperate for *just anyone's* attention.

Jesus cares about your learning to be content. Jesus knows what a "great gain" contentment is in the life of His girls. So, when your face another "friend-less" weekend, realize that this it is a chance for training in contentment through the strength and peace of Jesus.

The Secret of Contentment

If I were to tell you I had a secret code that would unlock a treasure chest and that I wanted to share with you all the treasure in it, well…wouldn't that be fabulous?! The thing is, I *do* know the secret that will bring you to a bounty of treasure, and it's given to us by the apostle Paul in his letter to the Philippians. Read this Scripture and pay close attention, because what Paul is sharing is that he learned to be *content in difficult circumstances* through the strength of Christ Jesus.

> *I am not saying this because I am in need, for I have learned to be content whatever the circumstances. I know*

what it is to be in need, and I know what it is to have plenty. I have learned the secret of being content in any and every situation, whether well fed or hungry, whether living in plenty or in want. I can do all this through him who gives me strength (Philippians 4:11-13 NIV).

Have you ever read about or heard what those difficult things were? You should read Second Corinthians 6:4-5, which lists just some of what Paul experienced. He was shipwrecked and beaten and went hungry and had all kinds of troubles that are hard to imagine. Yet through all those trials, he learned that *in Jesus*, he could do "all things." Now, read the verses again and pay even closer attention, because Paul is saying something else. He says that he has learned to be content when he has "plenty" and when he is "well fed." *What?* Who needs to learn contentment when life is full and all your needs are cared for?

Does that surprise or confuse you? I didn't understand that part of this Scripture when I first read it so many years ago. But let me tell you, I came to understand it! The Lord brought me and my husband into ministry with some people who were very wealthy and worked in their dream jobs. Many of them were professional baseball and football players who were in incredible shape and their wives were beautiful women. By the standards of the world around them, these people had *everything*. You know what I learned? First of all, that "everything" can cause a lot of stress for people. There's a lot to take care of and so many responsibilities.

Second, sometimes the more we have, the more we want! If a man can afford one luxury car, and he just loves having it, why not get another one…and another? Being able to have whatever you want means that there aren't external limits; you need to learn contentment to create internal limits. Finally, "everything" on the outside is absolutely no guarantee that *anything* on the inside is okay. Wealthy, successful, beautiful people can have as much heartache, sadness, and strife in their lives as anyone—it's just covered over by what looks so "perfect" on the outside.

So, people with plenty also need to learn about being content. And this is a lesson to us to be careful with those comparisons I wrote about. It may *look like* another person "has it all," but you may have no idea how discontent or unhappy they really are. The Bible tells us that the "secret to contentment" is that in every imaginable condition of life, when we turn to Jesus, He can teach us that He is *enough.* He is enough for the times we are struggling or in the midst of troubles, and He is enough for the times we seem to have all that we need.

Contentment and Unrealistic Expectations

In this letter to the Philippians, Paul was writing from *prison.* He was imprisoned for preaching the Good News

The Bible tells us that the "secret to contentment" is that in every imaginable condition of life, when we turn to Jesus, He can teach us that He is ***enough.***

of Jesus, sharing with people who were not imprisoned about a godly contentment that he had to learn. Isn't that remarkable? In the earlier verses of Philippians, chapter 4, Paul encourages us to do at least three things. He says to "Rejoice in the Lord!", He tells us to ask for what we need from God "with thanksgiving," and he describes what kinds of thoughts we should focus on in our minds (see Philippians 4:4-9). With these practices, it's clear that Paul learned to set his mind with gratitude and faith on the Lord—is it any wonder he learned the "secret to being content"? His relationship with Jesus is what taught him to be content.

If focusing on what's good and true, pure and just in this life brings about the peace of God, what is it that destroys peace in our hearts? I am convinced that, along with negative comparisons, our *expectations* can completely ruin any kind of peace or contentment. When we put all our mental energy into making up how we think things should go or what we "need" to have to be happy, we are basically preparing ourselves to be disappointed. Worse than that, we are preparing ourselves to be resentful!

Let's say you're going on a family trip to visit your cousins. You have so much fun with your cousins, and you think about all the things you'll do in their town—they belong to a swim club and there's an awesome outlet mall there. You love your aunt, especially, and one particular cousin who's only nine months older than you, and they always "spoil" you when you visit. The entire week before you leave and then your whole drive there, you build up the expectation of what you'll do and how people will treat you.

Now, skip ahead to the drive home. You are seething mad. You can't believe what a lame visit this was! Your oldest cousin is getting married soon and everyone was busy with all kinds of projects and planning. No one took you swimming or to the mall. Your aunt was distracted and your favorite cousin was paying more attention to her friend who came over to help than to you. Not only that, but they expected you to help! You spent the entire long weekend hot gluing flowers on garlands and rolling up meatballs to freeze. *Yuck!* Four hundred meatballs! You hate meatballs! Here, you gave up going to a party back at home just to get stuck being free labor for your aunt's family!

Can you feel your blood churning? What kind of attitude do you think you'll have in two weeks when you have to go back there for the wedding? Do you see how those *expectations*, the story in your head about what this trip would look like, were the exact thing that set you up to be so annoyed and resentful on the trip back home? I will confess to you, I have personally ruined more occasions for myself because of my unrealistic expectations of family and friends! What Jesus has taught me is that I need to give those expectations to Him. Psalm 62:5 says, *"My soul, wait silently for God alone, for my expectation is from Him"* (NKJV). Like Paul's encouragement to us in Philippians 4, when we bring our desires and hopes to Him in prayer and then notice and think *on purpose* about what is good in life, we find the peace of God. The peace of God is true contentment.

> *Rejoice in the Lord always. I will say it again: Rejoice! Let your gentleness be evident to all. The Lord is near. Do not be anxious about anything, but in every situation, by prayer and petition, with thanksgiving, present your requests to God. And the peace of God, which transcends all understanding, will guard your hearts and your minds in Christ Jesus.*
>
> *Finally, brothers and sisters, whatever is true, whatever is noble, whatever is right, whatever is pure, whatever is lovely, whatever is admirable—if anything is excellent or praiseworthy—think about such things. Whatever you have learned or received or heard from me, or seen in me—put it into practice. And the God of peace will be with you* (Philippians 4:4-9 NIV).

The Definition of Whining

Without looking, can you say what the very first word in this chapter was? I'll give you a hint—it started with the letter *w*. The word was "*Waaah!*" It was the sound of that unhappy baby. Babies often have good reasons to cry out. They don't have words, and they haven't yet learned that their needs will be taken care of. But what do we call it when a baby keeps crying after all her needs are met? *That* is a fussy baby. A fussy baby can be confusing and frustrating to a parent or babysitter, because you can't figure out how to calm her down. She just seems…discontent.

Well, babies aren't the only ones who can be fussy. Kids and adults have a way of expressing their disappointment and discontent, and it's called *whining.* When we are not content in our hearts, we have a very poor habit of whining and complaining. In the Bible, it's also called "grumbling" and "murmuring." Think back to the imaginary story about the trip to "your" cousins' house. Couldn't we add to that story that "you" were whining about the way things were going all weekend long as you faced disappointment after disappointment—and surely the loudest sound in the car on the way home were the moans of complaining and whining.

Years ago I heard a friend give a perfect definition of whining: "Whining is just anger squeezed through a tiny hole." People whine and complain when they are disappointed, when they are unhappy about how things are going. If disappointment simmers like water in a tea kettle, it can come to the boil of anger. Think about the tiny hole the steam of the boiling water goes through—what happens then? The steam pushed through that little hole makes a loud, piercing whistle. Have you noticed what can happen if no one is right next to the stove to turn off the heat? In my house someone practically *leaps* across the kitchen to turn off that annoying, screeching tea kettle! *This* is like the sound of whining—anger squeezed through a tiny hole.

Whining is the sound of a person wanting life to be exactly as he or she *wants it.* Whining is like the native language of me-centered people (which can be any of us from time to time). When things don't go just the way they want, it's a whining mess; it's like an accident scene of blame and complaining, criticism and sarcasm. You know what I think this kind of accident needs? A special kind of rescue vehicle that friends of mine used to call a *whambulance*—an ambulance for whiners! A "whambulance" comes to save people from "*Waaah! Waaah!*" When there's a mess of whining going on, someone needs to be rescued from their selfish wreckage. And seriously, the only cure the "whambulance" can bring is for people to learn that "secret of contentment" the Bible teaches us.

A No Whining Zone

Would your family describe you as one who whines a lot? I know parents who have girls who don't get into trouble in school or church and are good students with nice friends, but they are constant whiners. Here is a very serious warning: Whining may look innocent compared with causing trouble at school or stealing or being a bully, but let me tell you, the Word of God is very clear on what whining shows about one's heart. Jesus Himself teaches us in Luke 6:45:

> *A good man out of the good treasure of his heart brings forth good; and an evil man out of the evil treasure of his heart brings forth evil. For out of the abundance of the heart his mouth speaks* (NKJV).

The words we speak show us and others what's really going on in our hearts and minds. Oh, my young friend!

I so want you to have a heart *full of good treasure,* full of the good treasure Jesus died to give us in this life and the next. We don't want evil treasure overflowing from discontented hearts through our mouths. The "evil" Jesus warns about is unkind and ungrateful complaining that only tears other people down and offends God with our ungratefulness. The quality of our lives—how content and at peace we are—comes from the gratitude of our hearts. The heart that is ungrateful is almost always miserable.

So, would you describe your home as a No Whining Zone? Or is whining the 24/7 background music at your house? In our home, I would constantly say, "I can't hear you when you are whining!" Parents and daughters can create a No Whining Zone together by learning the serious effects of whining on one's life.

The Virus of Whining

One of the worst things about whining is that it is a habit. Not only a habit—whining is *contagious!* When you take the time to read in the Old Testament about the Israelites whining in the wilderness, the complaining began with only ten men and moved to *thousands* (see Numbers 13:32; 14:1-2; Joshua 14:8). The Lord was so displeased by the faithless whining of His chosen people that He disciplined them in the most harsh manner—thousands were killed there in the wilderness. I'm sure you can see why God would be so disturbed by their whining. They were complaining about

His plans for them; in fact, they were whining about His plan to deliver them from slavery in Egypt! We can roll our eyes at such ancient, faithless behavior, but we are not immune to this contagious behavior, I fear. If you start to pay attention, you will see that whiners tend to come in groups. Once someone begins complaining, it spreads to most of the people in the conversation.

Do you have a friend who encourages your whining or challenges your whining? Are you and your BFF like a "duet of whiners" who practices harmonies in the musical key of "W" for whining? I know that your parents have probably taught you not to use crude or rude speech, but have you also been taught to stop whining? Maybe our homes should have a *no whining jar.* The offenders would need to put in a quarter every time they whine. The money could be given away for missions!

You now know that whining is a habit, so let me encourage you that learning to be content is a great habit to replace it. My daughter's whining used to drive me crazy, until I realized that this "native language of whining" was learned from the other woman in the house—*me!*

Whining Versus Whatever

How can you overcome a habit of whining with a habit of contentment? How can you change one letter from "Waaah!" and get to "Aaah..."? When I saw the reflection of my own heart attitude in my little daughter, I began to study how serious whining is to the Lord and prayed that He show me the "evil treasure of my heart" that was causing it. I asked God for *a word* that would help remind me to resist the temptation to whine. One day I was reading about a teenager who said "Yes" in faith to an enormous task. Who was that teen girl and what was the huge job she said "Yes" to? Well, she was the brave "Shout Yes!" girl we looked at in Chapter 1—Mary, the mother of Jesus. If you get a chance to go back and read that section, you'll be reminded that I wrote about the "holy *whatever*" that Mary spoke. *Whatever* God's will was, she gave herself to it in total surrender. That was the word God gave me in answer to my prayer—*whatever.* To say "whatever" to God is the opposite choice to whining.

> *Mary responded, "I am the Lord's servant. May everything you have said about me come true"* (Luke 1:38 NLT).

Mary could have had no idea what was going to happen to her. Her response to the angel was her saying, "I am willing to accept *whatever* He wants." Training in contentment can be challenging, but by the power of the Holy Spirit, like young Mary, may you submit to God's process. This way, you can develop the holy habit of responding to the Lord with a holy "*whatever,*" even in response to disappointment and difficulties.

To say "whatever" to God is the opposite choice to whining.

Ruth, the P-31 Woman, and Contentment

I never get over how gracious our loving heavenly Father is to us through His Word. As I write this, I just shared with you about the young mother of Jesus, Mary, and now I get to show you some amazing connections between two other women in the Bible. Isn't God so thoughtful to give us girls so many women to relate to and encourage us in the Bible? Of course we learn from the men in the Bible, but it's just another proof of His loving kindness to His girls that He highlights girls and women, too!

The Book of Ruth is such a great story of a young woman learning contentment in a situation that would naturally produce whining. Because Ruth trusted in the God of Israel, she learned how to be content. Learning to be content grew in her the exact qualities that we see in the woman of Proverbs 31. Yes! That's the P-31 woman you read about in Chapter 2, "Diligence." I can't help but wonder whether the writer of Proverbs 31 was inspired by Ruth's awesome example. Ruth's inspiring story would have been passed from generation to generation. With Ruth being the great-great-grandmother of King David, it is very possible that her story was an influence on the writer of Proverbs 31. Take a look with me at the similar character strengths that describe both women:

1. Devoted to her family (see Ruth 1:15-18; Proverbs 31:10-12,23)

2. Delighted in her work (see Ruth 2:2; Proverbs 31:13)
3. Diligent in her labor (see Ruth 2:7,17,23; Proverbs 31:14-22,24,27)
4. Dedicated to godly speech (see Ruth 2:10,13; Proverbs 31:26)
5. Dependent on God (see Ruth 2:12; Proverbs 31:30)
6. Dressed with care (see Ruth 3:3; Proverbs 31:22,25)
7. Discreet with men (see Ruth 3:6-13; Proverbs 31:11-12,23)
8. Delivered blessings (Ruth 4:14-15; Proverbs 31:28,29,31)[2]

When I think about how much the Book of Ruth and Proverbs 31 have influenced me as a woman, I have to ask, "Wouldn't the above material be a great little Bible study for all of God's girls—not just this old lady!" Looking up these verses and seeing the character qualities that strengthened Ruth's contentment will certainly encourage you as a Young Lady of Contentment.

Notes

1. Horace Mann quoted in Richard A. Swenson, M.D., *A Minute of Margin*, (Colorado Springs: NavPress, 2003), front matter.

2. John MacArthur, *The MacArthur Daily Bible*, (Nashville: Thomas Nelson, 2003), 418.

Discussion Questions

Here are some questions you can think about or write about or talk about with someone else. It's not a test! So, feel free to look back in the chapter to help you think about your answers.

1. Why is Ruth such a strong example of contentment? (Consider what she was going through at the time.)
2. How can being content help you be patient and wait for God's best?
3. List some things that are causing you to be discontent. [after listing them, spend some time in prayer and ask God to help you to start being content in those specific areas.]
4. How can serving someone else and putting their needs before your own help you get over discontentment?
5. What does the Apostle Paul share about being content...*no matter what you are going through*? Phil.4:11,12
6. Describe the difference between "Whining" and "Whatever."

Chapter 9

Becoming a Young Lady of Conviction

Through Jesus' strength, you can stand firm, unwavering, as you wait for God's best. –JMK

Ruth's Convictions

Fairy tales are so much fun to read or see in a movie. It doesn't seem to matter if it's my four-year-old granddaughter or her "something-year-old" grandmother, we gals love a story with a princess and a knight in shining armor. Better than a fairy tale, though, is a *true* story of faith and love and courage, and the Book of Ruth is just that. It not only tells the story of a Lady in Waiting, but also draws the picture for us of her prince, the man of God's perfect choosing.

Ruth's choice to wait for God's best brought about her marriage to a Boaz rather than a Bozo. This admirable young woman did not allow the past influences of the heathen culture she grew up in to keep her from setting new standards and making wise choices that would honor God. She chose to break her family's sin cycle and begin a new, godly cycle. She married a man who was honorable, who honored her, and who was a pillar of strength. After they were married, she was blessed by having a son who would be included in the lineage of Jesus Christ. Ruth's wise choices led to her experiencing God's overwhelming goodness. Now, that's the best of tales!

In Chapter 4 you learned about the character trait of *virtue*, the moral excellence that helps a girl to make the best choices in life. Proverbs 31 tells us about a wife who is full of virtue, and in this chapter you will learn about the *convictions* that uphold virtue.

Conviction, as you may know, is a confident belief that stands behind our actions. When you have a conviction, you hold on tight to that belief, and you would go to great lengths to uphold it. A conviction is not easily shaken, either, unlike some things you may feel strongly about that can change. So, for example, a girl might *really* believe that mint chocolate chip is her *favorite* ice cream. It's all she ever gets when they go out for ice cream, and she is sure that she will be a mint-chocolate-chip girl for the rest of her life! But then…one day her brother dares her to try rocky road ice cream…and she loves it…and then she secretly gets her mom to buy it next time…and before the summer is over, her *new* favorite ice cream is *rocky road!*

You see, we can think or feel something strongly, with a lot of passion, even, but it still may not really be a conviction. Maybe you've heard the word *conviction* when people speak about their faith—"It is my conviction that Jesus Christ has died for my sins." Now, I stand on *this* belief in truth and I base my entire life on it. I certainly hope that you do, too! When we hold such faith convictions, they show through in our devotion to God and our diligence in serving Him. Virtue also comes from our faith convictions. In other words, because we love the Lord and believe that He loves and cares for us, we will want to know what *His* ways are. Therefore, when you commit yourself to godly ideas for dating and marriage, you will be able to say *no* when you need to and say *yes* to God's ways.

A Young Lady of Clear Convictions

As soon as you begin noticing the boys in your world, it is time to think about what your *convictions* are for dating and marriage. Like I've written before, you may be years away from dating, but convictions are the road signs on your journey to marriage that *guide* you along. Honestly, you are never too young to start building those convictions. Think about this: There were two ten-year-old girls, and one said,

*You may be years away from dating, but convictions are the road signs on your journey to marriage that **guide** you along. Honestly, you are never too young to start building those convictions.*

"I can't be bothered to think about things that aren't even going to *happen* until years and years from now. I just want to play and have fun." Then, that girl never gave another serious thought to what her dating ideals would be. The other girl said, "I want to learn what I can *now* so that when the time comes, I am the wisest I can be. I've seen some teens—and even adults—be broken-hearted in dating…and I want to prepare myself to make good choices." When those girls are 15 or 16, which girl do you think would be more likely to get confused by the attentions of a boy who was kind of a jerk? Which girl might hurt herself by going too far down that list we discussed in Chapter 6 on Purity? I know that you knew the right answer, because it's like anything else in our lives—to get ready for something prepares us for it. To be prepared means that fewer things take us by surprise.

Building your convictions now will help you choose wisely between the attention of a Bozo and the respect of a Boaz. It will help you be a better friend to your friends as they are making choices, and it will protect you from wasted time and broken-heartedness.

It's always incredible to me that teenage girls spend so much time getting "ready" for dates—the right outfit, right nail polish, right shoes, right hair accessory—yet spend *very little time* getting the most important part of themselves ready…*their hearts*. Long before the date, such readiness of heart, which is her conviction, should have influenced which guy she was attracted to and going out with in the first place!

So! Let's get right to it, Young Ladies of Conviction! Here is a list comparing the character of a Bozo and that of a Boaz. As you read it, you can begin to decide in your mind what traits you would want your husband to have. This is part of building your convictions for your future choices:

1. Bozo is controlled by his feelings.
   - Boaz controls his feelings. (He may get upset, but he knows what to do and what not to do with those feelings.)
2. Bozo is angered when he doesn't get his way.
   - Boaz can rise above disappointment; he knows God will give him peace.
3. Bozo doesn't notice the needs of others.
   - Boaz is courteous and aware of the needs of others.
4. Bozo is very critical of others and very intolerant.
   - Boaz is tolerant of imperfection because he knows that he isn't perfect, either.
5. Bozo is self-centered; he always wants life on his terms.
   - Boaz is others-centered, and therefore self-controlled.

6. Bozo is stubborn, and his viewpoint is the only "right" one.
    - Boaz is teachable; his heart and mind are open to what God would show him.

7. Bozo always makes excuses for not doing a task well.
    - Boaz strives to do his work to the best of his ability and to the glory of Jesus.

8. Bozo lacks integrity; he has no problem dishonoring a girl's purity.
    - Boaz has integrity and is committed to protecting a girl's purity.[1]

Phew! That's a big list with a lot being described! Don't worry, you can read it again and again. You can—and should—ask the Lord Jesus to help you see examples of these different things in the boys around you. Asking an older and wiser person for help to understand and to recognize these things is an excellent plan, too. And remember, you're not learning these things so that you can become critical of the boys around you. No! If you see "Bozo" behavior, it's best to go first to Jesus in your heart and pray for that boy to be changed. A really important thing you're learning in this book is to put up strong walls and keep a soft heart. The strong walls—convictions—keep you protected, while the soft heart—mercy—allows you to be kind to someone, even if you wisely keep your heart protected.

No Bozo Pajamas

Thirty years ago (I can hardly believe how long ago that is!) I was asked to speak at a meeting with many young, single ladies. The topic was "How to Avoid a Bozo." The young woman hosting the event had the cutest idea and had tee shirts made for all the gals at the meeting. On the front of the shirt, there was a drawing of the clown Bozo, set in a red circle, and crossing straight over his face was a diagonal, red line. Under the circle were the words "No Bozo!" Can you imagine how delighted I was to see those tees? They were fabulous! That tee shirt became my favorite display of my heart's message for all single daughters of the King.

I was so committed to my own daughter avoiding a Bozo for her future husband that when she was only four years old, once a week at least I would have her sleep in this "No Bozo" tee shirt. The funny thing was that little Jessi "hated" that shirt for some reason. But I would tell her, "Well, sweetheart, I hate Bozos and I love you," and continued to pull the shirt over her head. Just like I put her in that tee shirt when she was a tiny girl, I also began teaching her the principles I am teaching you in this book. Her young conviction of "No Bozo" helped her to wait on the Lord until she met the Boaz God had planned for her.

I continue to travel all over the country and I still use that 30-year-old "No Bozo" tee shirt as a visual aid in my talks. Unlike my four-year-old, people squeal with delight when they see it. The "No Bozo" tee shirt is a symbol of my passion to spread the word: *No Bozos* for our girls! You know what else? My sweet husband ordered me a car license plate with the words *No Bozo.* My passion is now displayed on my car everywhere I go!

Mentored by Hollywood

It's a true sadness to me how many boys are no longer being mentored by their fathers in godly character traits. Even for many grown men, the qualities of honor and purity are not held as convictions. I so hope that you have had a different experience with the men and boys around you. But let's be honest, boys as well as girls are often "babysat" and even mentored *by Hollywood.* What I mean is that busy parents "drop their kids off" at the TV or the computer screen and leave them there for hours. This ends up being how kids are learning about the opposite sex. Kids learn that what looks "normal" in movies or video games is what should be "normal" in real life. Don't get me wrong! My family has a *blast* watching movies! From the time my kids were little, we've always had a great time with each other watching all kinds of movies and shows. However, we watched them together so that we could talk about the message or the characters in the stories. Our entertainment was used by us to mentor our kids, it didn't do the mentoring.

More and more, movies and TV shows, video games and YouTube have added to the negative image of girls. In a show, when a boy is rude and hurtful to a girl, too often she thinks he is "just being a guy." If a girl has watched hours of TV where teen boys act foolishly and hurtfully, the girl thinks this is no more than normal teenage behavior. They don't even know there's something better! I am *so* grateful you're reading this book, because I know that *you* are a young lady who knows there is something better! Now, in the same way, boys play video games where even strong, fighting girls are dressed like they're in their underwear—with some fancy boots and a "kinda, sorta" coat that covers nothing—and that becomes the favorite picture in a boy's mind of what "female" is.

Is this a hopeless situation? Are all boys destined to be Bozo guys who only look at girls for their bodies? I am not willing to give in to this idea!

The second President of the United States was a man you probably have heard of. His name was John Adams, and he was one of the Founding Fathers of America. John Adams had a brave and strong wife named Abigail, whom he loved and often honored in public. A famous quote by Mr. Adams stated that the character of a nation's women was a huge influence on the morality and virtue of that nation. I have always found that interesting, as he was a man who respected his virtuous wife. His words also inspire me because he was a student of human nature and a very wise man. Because I know that human nature does not change a whole lot from generation to generation, I continue to have hope that Young Ladies of Conviction are a true *hope* for our nation.

I firmly believe, along with John Adams, that girls who actually have godly standards are one of the most important influences on our country's boys and young men. *You* are one of those girls! I know that because you are reading this book. Girls who act like princesses from God's unshakable Kingdom (not the entitled, selfish kind of princess from the Kingdom of Self) can be a powerful example to the guys around them, whether at school or youth group. Girls can set standards to live by that Hollywood long ago stopped modeling. And these standards, these actions of virtue, will help girls to not be "Bozo bait." Girls who are internally beautiful and who are Young Ladies of Conviction can affect their world enormously.

To influence change and inspire change is different than "making" someone change. I wrote about that in Chapter 4 on Virtue, especially. Remember those ninth-grade boys and their quiz? They knew that you can't force another person to change. Girls get confused and think that they can march right into a boy's life, get all tangled up in her own feelings, and then somehow her convictions will save her. But girls, one of your first convictions should be to *not* get tangled up with a Bozo. If you stand behind that wall to begin with, your strength of character will be an example to him. God may well use you to inspire change in a boy, but your responsibility is *to obey God and guard your heart*. Of course we want the boys to act like young men of honor, but for those who aren't getting that training, girls can be strengthened in the growth of their own convictions. Clear convictions give girls the courage to say *no* when a boy is unkind or inappropriate to her. *Girls who know how to say **no** are actually helping the boys to grow up!*

> *Of course we want the boys to act like young men of honor, but for those who aren't getting that training, girls can be strengthened in the growth of their own convictions.*

For some girls, saying *no* will be like learning a foreign language. However, a clear understanding of what Mr. Right and Mr. Wrong are like will help girls understand that "foreign" word. When girls can see the difference between Prince Charming and Prince Harming, they will be more confident to say *no* to Bozo guys! *Ha!* Don't you love that? "Prince Charming" and "Prince Harming." If you like to write stories or make videos, those are two characters you should use sometime! I'm smiling to myself just imagining them; although, in real life, there's nothing funny about Prince Harming!

The list above contrasting Boaz traits to Bozo ones is a great teaching aid in learning the difference between these characters. And the next list I'm going to tell you about is just as important!

Most Important List on Your iPad

When my niece was a young teen, her youth leader challenged her to make a list describing an ideal guy and to put that list in her wallet. She wrote out her list of what she felt was God's best version of a young man. My niece carried this list in her purse all through high school and college, and by God's grace, she went on to marry her own Mr. Wonderful. (Nowadays, girls can carry "the list" on their phones or tablets—though it's also good to keep a copy in your journal.)

The great wisdom in such an activity, writing out a list of excellent character traits, is that a young girl needs to decide *in advance* what a man worth waiting for is like. You don't decide in the moment when you're crushing on a guy. You decide in advance—before the hurricane of feelings overcomes you.

Years after my niece showed me her list, I met a girl who had just graduated from college. She also had a list describing the ideal guy. At the time I met this young woman, my husband, Ken, worked in a mission organization where a wonderful single guy was serving. This guy was everyone's crush. He was as wonderful inside as he was outside. I constantly heard comments about him from several young, single women, but part of what made him wonderful was that he was respectful of these gals, treating them "with all purity" as his sisters in Christ.

One day I asked the girl if she would be willing to share with me a few of the statements from her "Mr. Right" list. As she shared them, I couldn't help but think of that young man who served with my husband.

Here is what was on her list:

1. Spirit-controlled Christian
2. Jesus #1 in his life, not just an ornament
3. Broken: understands how to rely totally upon Jesus
4. Ministry-minded: wherever he is, he is available
5. Motivator: a man of vision, concerned about lost souls
6. Sensitive spirit: in tune to the needs of others
7. Understands the awesome responsibility of a husband to his wife
8. Humble enough to be a disciple (teachable) and able to disciple others
9. Man of prayer: knows the key to success is his private time with God
10. Family man: desires to have children and raise them properly for God's glory[2]

You may have guessed this by now, but the gal ended up dating the wonderful guy who worked with my husband. Not only did they date, they married—and they have been happily married for more than 20 years. Every year, when I see their Christmas card, I think of the girl with the list of her ideal guy. Her list helped her say no to Bozo guys, and it gave her clear convictions when her Mr. Right needed a *yes* from her.

Prince Charmings among Us

In 2007, I was getting ready to write another book and I sent out a survey of questions to a few hundred guys I knew. (Because I'd worked with pro athletes for 15 years, I knew *a lot* of guys!) The answers they gave were really so touching and inspiring. After reading them I thought: Deep in their hearts, men know God's ideals. They have the desire to be better guys, not Bozo guys. Guys need girls who have standards and convictions to remind them of those ideals deep in their hearts.

> *They show that the requirements of the law are written on their hearts, their consciences also bearing witness, and their thoughts sometimes accusing them and at other times even defending them* (Romans 2:15 NIV).

A Young Lady of Conviction can be a gentle but strong reminder of the God-given conscience that nudges young men to stop acting like Bozos. I'll tell you a real-life example of this happening.

While waiting for my time to speak at a conference, a young man came up to me. With the biggest smile on his face, he said, "I just want you to know, Mrs. Kendall, that I read your book."

Can you imagine my surprise? I was stunned. "Really? You read *Lady in Waiting*?"

"Yes ma'am, I have," he stated. "When my girlfriend broke up with me, she handed me *Lady in Waiting* and said, 'This is why I'm breaking up with you.'"

He went on to tell me how mad and in shock he was. He stormed back to his dorm room and threw the book down on his bed! But later on, when he was somewhat calmed down, he picked up the book and started to read it, out of curiosity. After all, think about it, if someone said, "This book explains the reason I rejected you," wouldn't you be kind of curious? I'm so glad he was curious and willing to look inside the book.

Then this young man said to me, "You know what the best part about reading that book was? Now I know what a *woman* worth waiting for is like."

That was great! Those words put a huge smile on my face. To know about a guy who was influenced to change his own standards by a Lady of Conviction was like being served a big ice cream sundae! But then he put the *cherry* on top of that sundae when he said, "All the guys I live with also read it." Fabulous! That made my day...my month! The fact that those college guys read a book written to young women about dating and marriage said to me that they were Prince Charmings in training.

Whether they are guys or girls, all of God's kids need to be trained the character qualities of truth, purity, patience, contentment, security, devotion, faith, and a passionate pursuit of Christ.

"The Lord Looks at the Heart"

Growing up, I noticed that I was always attracted to guys with dark hair and dark eyes; I had other friends who were liked boys with blonde hair and blue eyes. It's fine to have preferences, but our focus on just how a boy might look really showed how immature we were. The ideal guy each of us had in mind was only *external*; the idea was limited to what he looked like on the outside. Whenever I hear girls describing what their "perfect" guy looks like, I always ask, "What is his heart like? How does he treat those around him?" God's Word speaks loudly about looking only on outward appearances.

> *But the Lord said to Samuel, "Do not consider his appearance or his height, for I have rejected him. The Lord does not look at the things people look at. People look at the outward appearance, but the Lord looks at the heart"* (1 Samuel 16:7 NIV).

When my husband and I first met, he was *not* struck with love at first sight. In fact, his first thought was, "What in the world just walked into the Bible study!" I had just moved to South Florida from California, and I looked like the wildest hippie, with my very short dress and wire-rimmed glasses, long crazy hair, and the biggest Bible ever carried to a youth meeting!

My first thought when I saw Ken was, "This can't be the youth leader. He must be the pastor!" Ken's hair was very short and he was all dressed up, wearing a tie, and leading the youth Bible study. My youth leader in California didn't even own a tie, and he had long hair. Can you imagine if Ken and I had made our future decisions about each other based on what we looked like? We would never have married. He was blonde and blue-eyed—the opposite of what I normally was attracted to. I had dark hair and dark eyes—the opposite of his high-school sweetheart. *Ha!* Doesn't God have a sense of humor? He drew us to each other despite what we "thought" we were attracted to. How did that happen? It was our hearts toward Jesus that was the irresistible attraction for both me and Ken!

Every girl needs to think seriously about her image of what is *ideal* in a guy. And then she needs to bring that "must-have" list to God and lay it down before Him. Do you notice on the "Mr. Right List" above that there is not one word about the color of his hair or his eyes? Whenever my children would describe others as being "cute" or "hot," I would ask questions: "Are they kind? Do they love others? Are they generous? Are they giving?" I helped them to look past the surface to the heart qualities that were the *real* issue.

As you continue to learn and focus on what God looks upon in a person, you're building the firm foundation of your convictions for dating and marriage. You are never too young to pay attention. Watch and learn, girls, watch and learn! More than one famous love story is told from the view of a woman who first *watched* the young man and saw how he acted. One of my absolute heroes of the faith watched her big brother's friend from a distance for years before they ever talked about dating. Elisabeth Elliot paid attention to Jim and saw that he was kind to others, respectful of teachers and parents. He was a college guy who helped others and looked for ways to do that. He was a diligent student, and most important, his love of the Lord was contagious to all around him. By the time Jim noticed her and began to pay his attention to her, Elisabeth knew what a godly young man he was. Her convictions were *confirmed* in Jim, not challenged by him.

To be a Young Lady of Conviction is to be a princess *protected* behind the castle walls by her Father King. She is strong and brave and loving. When—and only when—the King puts down the drawbridge to invite a worthy prince inside the castle walls, is she truly meant to love.

Your convictions are your castle walls. Ask you Father God, the King Almighty, to help you build those walls, brick by brick.

Notes

1. The Bozo/Boaz comparison is adapted from subtitles in Chapter 6 of my book, *A Man Worth Waiting For* (Nashville: FaithWords, 2008).

2. List adapted from: Jackie Kendall and Debby Jones, *Lady in Waiting: Becoming God's Best While Waiting for Mr. Right* (Shippensburg, PA: Destiny Image, 2005), 129.

Discussion Questions

Here are some questions you can think about or write about or talk about with someone else. It's not a test! So, feel free to look back in the chapter to help you think about your answers.

1. How do your convictions impact your everyday actions and decisions?
2. Based on what you have read about Ruth, what are some of the convictions that she stood for?
3. Take this opportunity to write down some of your convictions—those confident beliefs that you build your life on. It's important to make this very clear.
4. Why is it so important to know what you convictions are *before* you start dating someone? Ruth 2:1-16
5. List out some of the convictions that you should have before dating someone. (it does not matter how old you are—the earlier and younger, the better. You need to settle your convictions before going into a relationship).
6. What convictions are you looking for *in a guy*? In a *friend*? Why do you think it's important that you have the *same convictions*?

Chapter 10

Becoming a Young Lady of Patience

Do you know what is worse than waiting?
Wishing you had. –JMK

Ruth's Patience

Ruth is a wonderful example of patience. She did not let her situation or her lack of a husband cause her to be angry or fed up—or to give up. Instead, she focused on her heavenly Father and chose to let Him bring her a husband as He saw fit. Perhaps Ruth was concerned about her "biological clock," but that didn't make her fearful of the future. Moving to a new country amongst hostile people and working in the fields with them didn't make her fearful, either. In faith, Ruth concentrated, not on getting a man, but on following the Lord and being a lady of character—such admirable character that we are still inspired by her almost 3,000 years later!

We can say from what the Bible tells us of Ruth's faith-filled behavior that she took life one day at a time, knowing that God was not limited by her situation or her age. I like the expression that "God's hands weren't tied." And through the process, she used the waiting time to become the woman God wanted her to be. Isn't this what we all want to be? The girls and the women God wants us to be? My heart's passion is for all of God's girls to wait for His best and for me to be used as His instrument to encourage their waiting, whether it is for a husband and family, a career, ministry, or any other calling of God.

My heart breaks, though, when I see again and again the impatience His daughters show in waiting on Him. Far too many young women act like God's hands *are* tied, and that if they don't take over and run the show, they'll never get what they want in their lives. One evening years ago I wrote a poem in response to yet another young woman marrying yet another Bozo guy who treated her poorly. She ended up with him because she had become impatient with God's plan for her life, and she settled for someone other than God's best.

This simple verse is my heart's cry for God's girls:

Don't Settle

I hope you don't consider me to meddle,
When I say don't settle.
Have you heard my heart scream?
Don't give up your dream.

So many have settled for Prince Harming,
Rather than courageously wait for Prince Charming.
Settling for a Bozo,
Whose heart will be a no-show.
Despairing over your absent knight in shining armor,
Will escort you into the arms of a carnival charmer.
Your Designer has dreamed much better for you,
Don't settle for a man who can't love you through and through.

Postponing Present Pleasure for Future Fulfillment

Now *that* heading is a good tongue-twister. Try saying that a few times, fast! And then say it again slowly, and think about what it means. These words are saying to *wait* for something nice you'd like to do *now*, some "present pleasure," in order to gain something better in the future. Learning how to "postpone" anything we want can be hard, whether it's eating a brownie or seeing a movie you're so excited about. Sometimes things like parties or vacations need to be postponed because of sickness or bad weather. No matter what, there can be a crying baby inside of us going "*Waaah!*" because we humans tend to *want what we want* ***when*** *we want it*. In our times, this idea of postponing pleasure is almost unheard of. We are the "fast food" and "instant access" generations.

I read an article in a magazine about how children are raised in France. I wonder if you know much about

France? The French *love* to eat, and they eat amazingly good food. Get this! It is a *law* in France that their butter and their chocolate must have a certain amount of fat—and it's a lot of fat! That extra fat means that French butter and chocolate and the yummy treats made with them are all the more fabulous! Well, if that's the case, why don't we see lots of overweight French people? I have often wondered about this...but then the article I read has given me a theory.

The author writes that from the time they are babies, French children are taught how to *wait.* School children are given one, small, healthy snack in the late afternoon and don't graze and snack throughout the day (oh my, I don't think they'd like my family's "Junk Food Drawer!"). Children in a restaurant are required to sit quietly and not run around. A woman the author interviewed said that the family is actually *trained* in putting off their pleasures. They are trained in self-control. My theory, having read this, is that such good training in "postponing present pleasure" gives those people the discipline to eat their wonderful foods in reasonable amounts and save certain things for special occasions. And because they learn this from such a young age, it's just what's *normal* to them.

When I read this, I couldn't help but think about how the *lack of patience* in my own country has led to so much obesity. The American blessing of abundance has also created an abundance of overweight people. This condition is at the opposite end of the chart from Hollywood's obsession with "body beautiful." But, isn't it interesting that we can turn on our TVs and be entertained by *America's Next Model*... *or* shows like *The Biggest Loser*? The diet and weight-loss business is worth billions of dollars! So, whether it's for thin women desperate to be even thinner, or obese people who are desperate to lose weight, that industry cashes in on the epidemic of impatience. What causes such a plague of impatience? It's the infection of discontentment. Being discontent causes people to impatiently go after what they think will "save" them.

Is *Wait* a Cuss Word?

Training in patience is actually not an option in life. It's a necessity for your security and happiness. Having to *wait* for things you really want develops not only patience but also self-control. This will bless absolutely every part of your future. What you learn about being patient as a 12-year-old—like being patient with your little brother or patiently waiting for your dad to help you with your homework—builds the muscles for a lifetime of patience. Because patience is required in life.

However, is the four-letter word *wait* like a cuss word to your ears? Does it make you want to cringe when you hear it? Whenever I speak to a teen gathering and say this four-letter word, *wait,* I always hear sighing and groaning rise up from the audience—and not from the moms in the crowd, but from the girls.

Waiting is necessary for God's best. And if God's best is a husband, then waiting on God is the best plan for you to find a Boaz. On the other hand, *impatience* is the easiest way to find a Bozo. So when the young girls I speak to moan and groan when they hear the word *wait,* I make sure to give them an important *reality check*. I ask them this question: "What is worse than waiting?"

As the girls start to think how to respond, I blurt out my answer: "Wishing you had!" What is *worse* than waiting is wishing you had waited! Worse than the sometimes difficult discipline of patience is...regret! Is there anything you ever wished you had waited for? Did you ever push someone to tell you what a surprise gift was because you didn't want to wait...and then the surprise wasn't so much fun? What about when someone doesn't wait and tells another person about her surprise? That definitely causes regret, ruining someone's surprise. I have spent decades counseling all those ladies who *wished* they had waited for their Boaz.

God's Patient Heart

Why do you think those teen girls respond to the idea of patiently waiting with a groan? Why would the word *wait* hit their ears like a curse? I believe it's because so many people haven't really learned what "patience" means and why it is a good thing. And if there is anything I most want to do in this final chapter it's to encourage you in the hopeful peace of patience. I want you to finish reading this chapter with a fresh understanding that gives you renewed strength and *joy* in waiting. Yes! To postpone pleasure and delay delight can indeed be done with *joy!*

The very first and most important thing for you to know is that patience is at the core of who God is. Therefore, to grow as a Young Lady of Patience is to grow in the character of our Lord and Savior. This is our greatest goal as Christians, to work with God's Holy Spirit and become more like Him—so let's see what the Bible tells us about God's patience.

To grow as a Young Lady of Patience is to grow in the character of our Lord and Savior.

I'm going to dive in to a little word study to help you learn about patience, because I've realized over the years that lots of people only think of patience as a *passive* activity. They think it just means to grit their teeth and put up with something and that maybe, magically, they'll feel a kind of peaceful feeling. You can imagine a kind mother comforting a child's frustration by saying, "Shhh, sweetie, be patient." Or, on the other hand, an angry parent may bark at a nagging child, yelling, "Just be *patient!*" But chances are that few people are taught *how* or really *why* to be patient.

What the Bible tells us, over and over again, is that God is patient with us. Here is a verse describing that truth:

And he passed in front of Moses, proclaiming, "The Lord, the Lord, the compassionate and gracious God, slow to anger, abounding in love and faithfulness (Exodus 34:6 NIV).

Note the term "slow to anger," because that's the term in both Old Testament Hebrew and New Testament Greek that means "patience." It means that one's temper is delayed and not acted upon. God does that because He is *full* of love for us. God chooses to put His anger off and to display his grace and faithfulness toward us. This word is used 28 times in the Bible to reassure us that *God is patient!*

In fact, when the Lord tells us through Paul's writing about what *love* looks like, the true love inspired by God's character, look at the first adjective used to describe it:

Love is patient and kind; love does not envy or boast; it is not arrogant or rude. It does not insist on its own way; it is not irritable or resentful (1 Corinthians 13:4-5 ESV).

There, you see? Love is patient...God calls us to be patient, because He is patient and it's a quality of great value to Him.

You can also see in these verses some characteristics of impatience. Insisting on our own ways, being irritable and resentful—that sure sounds like impatience to me. A person gets irritable and whines when she doesn't get her own way. She might even become resentful or bitter. Those states of mind grow because we practice thoughts over and over in our heads like, "It's not fair!" and "I can't believe this isn't going the way I wanted it to!" We fan the flame of being annoyed and angry with thoughts like that, which is the opposite of not acting upon those intense feelings. But imagine if we step out of the me-centered demands for things to go how we want, for things to happen in our own time frames. Imagine if we *stop* the selfish and fearful thoughts and don't give any more fuel to that fire? I'm so excited to tell you two things now: *why* and *how* to do that.

As you commit to become more like Jesus in this patience training, you actually encourage the Lord to act in your life. How do I know this? Here's a verse from the prophet Isaiah describing our one and only God in this way:

> *Since ancient times no one has heard, no ear has perceived, no eye has seen any God besides you, who acts on behalf of those who* ***wait*** *for Him* (Isaiah 64:4 NIV).

To "wait" in this Scripture means to "stay seated." Patience is to remain seated, trusting God with what you need, instead of standing with your hand on your hip and your toe tapping the floor impatiently! Our heavenly Father knows what is best for us and wants us to grow in our trust of Him. When we wait for Him, we *bless God*. When we wait for Him, we are saying to God, "I know You love me and I have faith in You." By "staying in our seats" we show Him our total surrender to His perfect plan.

That's the heart and mind attitude that is most ready for the next step in the journey; and when God knows we are ready, He acts. I'll tell you this, girls, I want God's plan and His ways, because I have learned again and again that it's the best plan. So, if learning to wait on Him makes that happen—sign me up!

Let's review *why* you want to learn patience: 1) It is a character trait of God's love, and 2) He promises us He works for those who wait on Him.

Patience Power

You might be thinking, "I really do want to follow Jesus with a good attitude...but sometimes it's just so hard to be patient!" You're right! It can be a real challenge, especially if you have a familiar habit of complaining or being discontent. But here is good news right from the heart of Jesus: He knows that we are weak. He knows that we can *only* be patient and kind, faithful and loving in *His power.* And His Word reminds us to come to Him for that power.

Looking to Jesus for the power to be patient is the secret weapon of *how* to grow in patience.

I want you to look at the following verses and notice the little word "for." Paul is praying that the believers in Colossae would be given power *for* patience.

> *May you be strengthened with all power, according to his glorious might, for all endurance and patience with joy, giving thanks to the Father…* (Colossians 1:11-12 RSV).

If patience were an easy thing to come by we would not need the power of Almighty God to get it! In fact, there are *three* different "power" words in this one, short verse—*strength*, *power*, and *might*. I would say that God is making His point loud and clear!

Now, I want you to see that this verse uses two different words to describe patience. The word translated as "patient" is mostly used to mean patience with *people*. The word right before it, in Greek, means to be patient in *situations*. Here, this word is translated as "endurance." In some Bibles it's translated as "perseverance." To *endure* is to stick with something, to wait it out; and to *persevere* is to press on or push through and keep going. We must be patient to endure and to persevere, and we need the power of God to do that. So, for you to think that patience can be difficult for you, *you're right!* It's exactly the kind of attitude that we cannot hold on to very well for very long without being empowered by God.

Let's keep looking at this verse just a little more, because it shows us another golden nugget of truth—and the Scripture is full of those, isn't it? It really is a treasure chest! Along with Patience Power, Paul prays for that patience to come with *joy*. Wow! Is that truly possible? To be joyfully patient? The Word of God tells us that it is, and it even tells us what to do to experience that joy: "Give thanks to the Father." When we are thankful to God, we set our minds and hearts on what is *good*. We can't be thankful to God and stay cranky for too long. A heart that is thankful to the Lord finds joy, which is exactly how our patient endurance can be joy-filled. Patience is an unlikely path to joy.

Giving thanks when you want to be cranky can actually transform you from a whiner to a willing worshiper!

Training our gratitude muscles with Patience Power can happen every single day. Is your sister taking too long in the bathroom? The second you start to feel the annoyance creeping up your neck, you can *stop* and pray, "Lord Jesus! I need Your power right now to be patient!" and then think about things to *thank God* for. In that very moment you can thank God for your heart beating and for the breath that keeps you alive. You can thank Him for His perfect love and for His sacrifice for you on the cross. You can thank God for *a bathroom*—knowing there are people all over the world who don't have a nice bathroom of their own. Once you choose to thank the Lord in faith, you will find that fussy impatience starts to fade away. After all, you've got to wait for the bathroom anyway, why not give God that time and praise and thank Him? Giving thanks when you want to be cranky can actually transform you from a whiner to a willing worshiper!

That example might seem a little goofy to you, but there is absolutely no situation too small to pray to Jesus about and no time wasted when we turn our minds toward Him. Practicing patience and seeking His power in the small things is the training that prepares us for the longer, more difficult endurance that we will face in life. The patience that develops in your heart will allow you to wait for "true love." For true love it's necessary to be mature and committed, and impatience has no tolerance for that.

Do You Have a Spiritual Monitor?

Patience was the red carpet that Ruth walked down to receive God's best for her—Boaz, a man worth waiting for. I am sad to report that I have seen thousands of precious girls miss the red carpet to God's best because of their unwillingness to wait. You can be sure that every good choice you make now to choose gratitude and patience will prepare you to receive God's best—a Boaz instead of a Bozo.

The pressure for dating and "romantic" relationships with boys begins at younger and younger ages. Crushes and peer pressure that may have begun in sixth or seventh grade a generation ago now occur in third or fourth grade—that's your age or even younger! By the time a girl is in high school and allowed to go out on dates, she has been surrounded by a boy-crazy culture for years! At that point, the longer she is dateless, the more impatient she can be waiting for "Mr. Right."

In Chapter 4 when you read about virtue, do you remember what it was that could cause "toothpicks in your eyes"? *Ha!* I hope that image stuck with you. You were learning how important it is to not date or marry a guy who is not following Jesus. Well, girls who settle for Bozo guys or even very nice non-believers are showing the world their impatient hearts. Me-centric girls do not know how to be patient, and their desire for instant delight often means they attach themselves to Bozo guys!

Long before such an attachment was made, this young woman began noticing boys. Girls notice boys. This is a normal experience. For a girl to begin to focus and think about the boy she has noticed is not unusual. But we've talked a lot in this book about what repeating thoughts can lead you to. Like Molly daydreaming about Tyler, and the "Law of Diminishing Returns," too many of the wrong kinds of thoughts make a girl's impatience worse. Before she knows it, she is much more connected in her mind and heart than she should be at all.

So, here's a big question: Do you have someone older and wiser, someone you can share with about a guy whom you might be crushing on? It might be your mom or a Sunday school teacher or a girl youth leader. A *spiritual monitor* will listen to you describe the cute guy you are attracted to and then she will ask wise questions. Of course you need to bring your thoughts and feelings to the Lord, but the Lord gives us one another to help each other; and this is an area of our lives we all need support in.

Sometimes my daughter's friends would mention a cute guy at school. As I would listen to the teens, I would look for a chance to ask the girls what they like most about this particular guy. I would ask for reasons why he stands out among all the other boys. Too often the descriptions were all externals—hair, eyes, smile, height, and even a cool car! I would then ask, "Is he a Christian?" And far too often the answer I would hear was, "Um…I'm not really sure!" Usually, though, just asking that question would cause my daughter's young friend to begin thinking about the most important things to consider when noticing a certain guy.

I have a friend who came home from a date and was so excited she was talking a hundred miles an hour to her mother about this wonderful guy and the perfect evening they had together. Her mother was a wise woman and a spiritual monitor for her two daughters. Her reply to her daughter's giddy excitement was, "Kimmy, sweetie, you need to settle down a little bit. Don't go buy a bride's magazine. Don't already name your children. You've had one date, OK?"

Now, her mom's reply may seem extreme, but girls and women alike move fast in the area of emotional attachments. A precious teen who's had one date with a guy can already be dreaming about going to the senior prom with him—and they are both only freshmen. Maybe you're thinking, "Are you kidding me?" But some of you know what I am talking about. I had a crush on a guy in fifth grade, and I constantly wrote my first name and his last name on my school folder—Jackie Burke! That might sound "cute" or "perfectly innocent" to you, but those silly little crushes morph into bigger crushes. Too often, without a spiritual monitor a girl can get herself into some emotional—as well as physical—trouble.

A spiritual monitor is like the part of a car's gas pedal that limits how hard you can press it down. That's called a "governor." It protects the driver from pushing too hard and making the car rocket ahead too fast. Well, a wise, older woman can be a governor for a girl's emotional gas pedal, keeping the "love mobile" from speeding into the arms of a Bozo. I sure hope you have someone older whom you respect, who can share your joys and dreams with you. Do you have such a person in your life right now? If not, ask Jesus to give you someone wise to listen to your heart's crushes. This person is willing to pray for you that you will grow as a Young Lady of patience and learn patience with joy.

I am constantly cheering for girls to be patient and not run ahead of God's plan. Whether the girl is a freshman in high school or freshman in college, all girls need a spiritual monitor to help guard her heart and guide the direction of her focus.

> *He who walks with wise men will be wise, but the companion of fools will suffer harm* (Proverbs 13:20).

Choose Your Words Carefully

The words we use to describe things are very important. If a surgeon is in the middle of heart surgery and says to the nurse, "Please hand me the thingamajig," do you think that nurse will be likely to hand him the right instrument? What if you shared a favorite game with your siblings, but every time you thought of playing it or spoke of it, you called it "*my* game"? Can you see how calling it "my" game instead of "our" game would cause you to think about it differently? You might get annoyed when someone else took it out of the closet to play or you would think they needed to ask your permission.

The words we use to describe things definitely affect us. Knowing this fact, my husband and I made it a point to teach our daughter (and some of her girlfriends) the best term to describe a boy they might know and enjoy being around. He was not a "boyfriend" but a "friend who is a boy." That simple difference in words helped put a boundary around how the girls talked about and even thought about the boys they knew. It became another kind of heart guard that protected them from the boy-crazy environment surrounding them.

We used this explanation so often around our house that I would often hear our daughter's friends say, "He is not a *boyfriend*, he is a *boy who is a friend*." Any time I heard that I just praised Jesus! I knew that helping our daughter and her friends learn a holy habit like this would strengthen them in Patience Power. They didn't "zoom ahead" by thinking of a friend as a "boyfriend" and getting their hearts ahead of where a friendship really was. Practices like this protected them throughout high school and college and even after! Most of her close girlfriends have married a prince of a guy!

One time I got a letter that a sixth-grader had written after being heartbroken by her "breakup" with a boy whom she had been "in love with" since fourth grade. Not only did she consider him her "boyfriend," but she used all kinds of words that were completely inappropriate for a 12-year-old. The words written in the letter disturbed me deeply, *because the emotions were so exaggerated compared to the reality of the relationship.* The letter sounded like an adult woman who had been married for years and then been betrayed by her husband. This precious young girl hadn't had a spiritual monitor who could help her tame her emotions during those years. As a 10- and 11-year-old, this girl already got her heart so tangled up with a young boy that she was *crushed* at 12 when she woke up to the reality of the friendship.

Don't Get Crushed by Your Crush

I know that girls crushing on boys is normal, but it can cause you to *get crushed*, too. This passionate heartbreak letter by a sixth-grader fueled my heart's fire to keep warning girls.

It is dangerous to fan the flames of passion in your heart before you are mature enough to handle the emotions.

And beware, girls! It is just as dangerous to blow on that fire in your friends' hearts. Part of your patience training includes *holding your tongue* when it comes to other girls' crushes. Every time girlfriends chatter with excitement about the attention a girl gets from a boy, they throw wood on the fire of her heart. "Oh my gosh! I saw him staring at you in class!" and "I am *so* sure he's into you, 'cause he always goes out of his way to pass your locker." Comments like these may *feel* fun and exciting to make, but they are of no real help to your friend! You are most wise and most loving to help her stand behind the castle walls of conviction by resisting the urge to say things like this. Even better, you can encourage your friend to pray for the boy, just like you've been learning. Sometimes, honestly, the best thing you can do is to change the subject!

Every single principle I have shared with you in the pages of this book will be greatly supported if you and your friends are on the same team.

I am hoping that your BFF and your closest circle of girlfriends are fellow Christians who "work out" together in your training of patience. Every single principle I have shared with you in the pages of this book will be greatly supported if you and your friends are on the same team.

There is a lot to learn, I know; so if you've read this book on your own, why not plan to read it again with a friend or a few friends? Each of you, along with your moms and other spiritual monitors in your lives, can build one another up, like the Scripture says:

> *But encourage one another day after day, as long as it is still called "Today," so that none of you will be hardened by the deceitfulness of sin* (Hebrews 3:13).

Being a Young Lady in Waiting

I wonder if you find "good-byes" as sad as I do. Even if I trust the Lord for His plans and have every hope to see a friend again, saying good-bye after a long and delightful visit is hard. That's how I am feeling now as I write the final pages of *Waiting for Your Prince.* I wish that we were sitting together up on the edge of a beautiful castle wall, looking out at the enormous countryside. Such an expanse of green hills and maybe an ocean in the distance—it's a landscape of hope! You never know what ship might come to port or what band of merry friends might come galloping over the hill. There is so much in your life to look forward to. You have every good reason to wait on the Lord with excitement for what He has for you.

By the time you have come this far and at the last page here, you have certainly shown that you *are* becoming a

Young Lady of Patience, because it takes patience *and* diligence to get through an entire book like this. Sitting on that castle wall, I would tell you how very *proud I am of you!* And as I ride away in my carriage, after we gave each other a big hug, you would turn around and see that I have left you a present. It's a banner made of satin and velvet that's as big as the castle door. The banner hangs on the wall from a thick, gold rod with elaborate carvings on each end. The banner's words are embroidered and embellished in all your favorite colors; and here is what they say—to remind you of everything you have learned in the journey of this book.

Waiting for Your Prince *is not about finding the right man,*
but becoming the right woman.
A Young Lady in Waiting
totally surrenders *herself to the Lordship of Christ,*
diligently *uses her days,*
trusts God with growing ***faith,***
demonstrates ***virtue*** *in daily life,*
loves God with focused ***devotion,***
stands for physical and emotional ***purity,***
lives in ***security,***
responds to life with ***contentment,***
makes choices based on her ***convictions,***
and waits ***patiently*** *for God to meet her needs.*

Note

1. Pamela Druckerman, "Why French Parents Are Superior," *The Wall Street Journal*, wsj.com, February 4, 2012, http://online.wsj.com/article/SB10001424052970204740904577196931457473816.html (accessed September 21, 2012).

Discussion Questions

Here are some questions you can think about or write about or talk about with someone else. It's not a test! So, feel free to look back in the chapter to help you think about your answers.

1. How can *not* being patient lead you to make poor choices?
2. In what ways does your self-security and faith in God help you stay patient?
3. Think about this. How can one moment or decision of impatience totally change your life? Do you know of anyone that this has happened to?
4. How is self-control a good thing? [especially, how can self-control protect you from making harmful decisions and getting into bad relationships?]
5. Do you have a spiritual monitor in your life? If so, who is she? If not, pray for God to lead you to this person.
6. Since so many people think *patience* is a bad thing, I want you to take this moment to write down every *blessing* of patience that you can think of. Remember, faith is about believing that God exists and that He is a rewarder of those who seek Him. Isaiah 64:4

   Write down some of the *rewards of patience*...

About Jackie Kendall

Jackie Kendall is president of Power to Grow Ministries. She is a national conference speaker and the best-selling author of *Lady in Waiting, The Mentoring Mom, A Man Worth Waiting For, Free Yourself to Love: The Liberating Power of Forgiveness,* and *Lady in Waiting for Little Girls.* She has been married 40 years to Ken and they have two grown children, Ben and Jessi, and three grandchildren.